THE **India** A-Z
Quiz Book

Derek O'Brien was born in Kolkata. He began his career as a journalist for *Sportsworld* magazine but soon shifted to advertising. After working for a number of very successful years as Creative Head of Ogilvy, Derek decided to focus all his energy and talent in his passion—quizzing.

Today, Derek is Asia's best-known quizmaster and the CEO of Derek O'Brien & Associates. He has been the host of the longest-running game show on Indian television, *The Cadbury Bournvita Quiz Contest*, for which he was voted the Best Anchor of a Game Show at the Indian Television Academy Awards for three years in a row. Always innovating, Derek is also credited with having conducted the first quiz on Twitter in 2010.

Derek has written over fifty bestselling reference, quiz and textbooks. In 2011, he was elected to the Rajya Sabha as a Member of Parliament (MP) and is the Leader of the All India Trinamool Congress Parliamentary Party in the Rajya Sabha and the chief national spokesperson of the party.

Keep in touch with Derek on Twitter, where his handle is @quizderek, and on Facebook at www.facebook.com/MPDerekOBrien/

Other books by Derek O'Brien
(published by Rupa Publications)

The Bournvita Quiz Contest Quiz Book 2012
Bumper Bournvita Quiz Contest Quiz Book
Derek Introduces 100 Iconic Indians
Derek Introduces the Constitution and Parliament of India
Derek's Challenge
My Way: Success Mantras of 12 Achievers
Speak Up Speak Out
The Best of Bournvita Quiz Contest
The Bournvita Quiz Contest Quiz Book 2014
The Bournvita Quiz Contest Quiz Book 3
The Bournvita Quiz Contest Quiz Book 2017
The Essential BQC Quiz Book
The Ultimate Bournvita Quiz Contest Book of Knowledge Volume 1
The Ultimate Bournvita Quiz Contest Book of Knowledge Volume 2
The Ultimate Bournvita Quiz Contest Book of Knowledge Volume 3
The Ultimate Bournvita Quiz Contest Book of Knowledge Volume 4
The Ultimate Winning Minds Quiz Challenge
The School Quiz Book
Challenge Your Mind: The Very Best of Derek O'Brien

THE India A-Z Quiz Book

DEREK O'BRIEN

RUPA

Published by
Rupa Publications India Pvt. Ltd 2017
7/16, Ansari Road, Daryaganj
New Delhi 110002

Sales centres:
Allahabad Bengaluru Chennai
Hyderabad Jaipur Kathmandu
Kolkata Mumbai

Copyright © Derek O'Brien & Associates 2017

All rights reserved.
No part of this publication may be reproduced, transmitted,
or stored in a retrieval system, in any form or by any means, electronic,
mechanical, photocopying, recording or otherwise, without the prior
permission of the publisher.

ISBN: 978-81-291-4827-8

Sixteenth impression 2022

20 19 18 17 16

The moral right of the author has been asserted.

Printed in India

This book is sold subject to the condition that it shall not, by way of
trade or otherwise, be lent, resold, hired out, or otherwise circulated,
without the publisher's prior consent, in any form of binding or cover
other than that in which it is published.

For Dilip Chatterjee.
Thank you for trusting me to conduct a national-level quiz when I was just twenty-six.

CONTENTS

Amazing India (Places to See)	1
Blue Chip (Businesses)	7
Connecting India (Communications)	13
Dressing Up (Clothes and Accessories)	19
Enabling India (Organizations)	25
Full Toss (Cricket)	31
Gourmet (Food)	37
Housefull (Films)	43
Incredible India (Mixed Bag)	49
Jukebox (Music)	55
Know All (Potpourri)	61
Landscape (Geography)	67
Mixed Bag	73
Next-Door Neighbours (Neighbouring Countries)	79
Outstanding Performances (Awards)	85
Play Off (Sports)	91
Quill Pen (Literature)	97
Remarkable Women (Indian Women)	103
State of the Art (Art and Culture)	110

Take Off (Travels)	116
Unity in Diversity (Fairs and Festivals)	122
Voices (Quotes by Famous People)	128
Wilderness (Wildlife)	135
X-Factor (Unique Feats)	141
Yesterday, Once More (History)	147
Zero Hour (Parliament and the Constitution of India)	153
Answers	159

AMAZING INDIA

1. Which monument had its principal mausoleum completed in AD 1648 and its outlying buildings and gardens finished 5 years later in AD 1653?
   a) Gol Gumbaz
   b) Bibi Ka Maqbara
   c) Taj Mahal
   d) Humayun's Tomb

2. A ruler of which dynasty laid the foundation of the Qutb Minar?
   a) Tughlaq
   b) Sayyid
   c) Lodi
   d) Slave

3. In which of these landmarks would you find a tank or pool called the Amrita Saras?
   a) Red Fort
   b) Golden Temple
   c) Brindavan Gardens
   d) Jantar Mantar

4. Within which of the following complexes in Hyderabad would you find the oldest mosque of the city?
   a) Charminar
   b) Qutb Shahi Tombs
   c) Chowmahalla Palace

d) Golconda Fort

5. The legend of Bishu Maharana and his son—who after completing the final work on this monument, jumped to his death—is associated with...
   a) Sun Temple, Konark
   b) Golden Temple, Amritsar
   c) Lotus Temple, New Delhi
   d) Kamakhya Temple, Guwahati

6. Which monument, located at 1 Queen's Way, was built not only as a memorial for a queen but also as a national gallery and Valhalla of the Indian Empire?
   a) Victoria Memorial
   b) Bibi Ka Maqbara
   c) Gol Gumbaz
   d) Taj Mahal

7. Which city would you be visiting if you were looking at Veiled Rebecca, a marble statue acquired by Salar Jung I from Rome in 1876?
   a) Kolkata
   b) Chennai
   c) Hyderabad
   d) Mumbai

8. Where would you be if you have arrived by a toy train at the highest railway station in India?
   a) Mughalsarai Junction Railway Station
   b) Dudhsagar Railway Station
   c) Chhatrapati Shivaji Maharaj Terminus
   d) Ghoom Railway Station

9. Where did Emperor Ashoka erect the Great Stupa after the redistribution of mortal remains of Lord Buddha?
   a) Kushinagar
   b) Sarnath
   c) Sanchi
   d) Bodh Gaya

10. Which structure was built at Apollo Bunder to commemorate the visit of King George V and Queen Mary to Mumbai?
    a) Gateway of India
    b) Town Hall
    c) Chhatrapati Shivaji Maharaj Terminus
    d) Mumbai High Court

11. Originally built in 1143 on a hilltop under the reign of the Raja of Warangal, this mud fort was then known as Mankal. Name the fort.
    a) Vellore Fort
    b) Fort William
    c) Red Fort
    d) Golconda Fort

12. Name the important urban centre of ancient Odisha which was popularly known as Arkakshetra or Padmakshetra.
    a) Konark
    b) Puri
    c) Jajpur
    d) Balasore

13. Which fort in Rajasthan did Rudyard Kipling refer to as 'the work of giants'?
    a) Mehrangarh Fort
    b) Amer Fort
    c) Kumbhalgarh Fort
    d) Jaisalmer Fort

14. The temples at Khajuraho belong to 2 different religions. One of them is Hinduism. Which is the other one?
    a) Buddhism
    b) Jainism
    c) Sikhism
    d) Bahá'í Faith

15. Which famous landmark houses the Durbar Hall, the Ashoka Hall and the Mughal Gardens?
    a) Rashtrapati Bhavan
    b) Victoria Memorial
    c) Mysore Palace
    d) Fatehpur Sikri

16. Vimal Vasahi, dedicated to Adinath, is the oldest temple of which of the following?
    a) Jaipur City Palace
    b) Ajanta and Ellora Caves
    c) Dilwara Temples
    d) The temples at Khajuraho

17. Which fort did Emperor Babur describe as 'the pearl amongst the fortresses of Hind'?
    a) Mehrangarh Fort

b) Old Fort
   c) Red Fort
   d) Gwalior Fort

18. Which present-day Indian state houses the Group of Monuments at Pattadakal?
    a) Andhra Pradesh
    b) Tamil Nadu
    c) Kerala
    d) Karnataka

19. Once a great monastic-cum-educational centre, this ancient city was the birthplace and the land of nirvana of the great Buddhist monk Sariputta. Name this place.
    a) Nalanda
    b) Sarnath
    c) Bodh Gaya
    d) Kushinagar

20. The mausoleum of which Mughal emperor is located at Sikandra, a place named after Sikandar Lodi?
    a) Babur
    b) Humayun
    c) Akbar
    d) Jehangir

21. Built between 1786–91 by Nawab Asaf-ud-Daula, its central hall is said to be the largest-vaulted chamber in the world. Name the monument.
    a) Bara Imambara
    b) Tomb of Itmad-ud-Daula

c) Khas Mahal
　　d) Agra Fort

22. Which of the following forts in Rajasthan is also known as 'Sonar Quila'?
    a) Chittorgarh Fort
    b) Amer Fort
    c) Jaisalmer Fort
    d) Kumbhalgarh Fort

23. Which of these temples is located on top of a hill called Neelachal Parbat or Kamagiri in Guwahati?
    a) Kamakhya Temple
    b) Golden Temple
    c) Kalighat Temple
    d) Kashi Vishwanath Temple

24. Which of these monuments was built by Sawai Pratap Singh in 1799 as a summer retreat for him and his family?
    a) Agra Fort
    b) Golconda Fort
    c) Hawa Mahal
    d) Gol Gumbaz

25. The foundation stone of which monument, designed by Edwin Lutyens, was laid by the Duke of Connaught in 1921?
    a) India Gate
    b) Gateway of India
    c) Victoria Memorial
    d) Chhatrapati Shivaji Maharaj Terminus

BLUE CHIP

1. Which king of the Solar Dynasty paid back his debts to Vishwamitra by selling his wife, Chandramati, his son and himself?
   a) Harishchandra
   b) Maharana Pratap
   c) Parikshit
   d) Bhagiratha

2. The national anthem of which country was composed on a ship called the *Minden* built by the Wadia Group?
   a) USA
   b) Portugal
   c) France
   d) Bangladesh

3. The logo of Air India is a flying red swan with the '____' in orange placed inside it. Fill in the blanks.
   a) Gateway of India
   b) Taj Mahal
   c) Konark Chakra
   d) Ashokan Pillar

4. Who, along with Gary Hamel, introduced the concept of Core Competence in the *Harvard Business Review*?
   a) Sumantra Ghoshal
   b) C.K. Prahalad

c) Ram Charan
d) Vijay Govindarajan

5. What is the name of the mobile app developed by National Payments Corporation of India (NPCI) based on the Unified Payment Interface (UPI)?
    a) BHIM
    b) ARJUN
    c) KRISHNA
    d) INDRA

6. The title of which book by Rashmi Bansal is taken from Steve Jobs' commencement address at Stanford University in 2005?
    a) *Follow Every Rainbow*
    b) *Stay Hungry, Stay Foolish*
    c) *Poor Little Rich Slum*
    d) *Connect the Dots*

7. In India, the first photo exhibition by Instagram explored which state?
    a) Maharashtra
    b) Andhra Pradesh
    c) Goa
    d) West Bengal

8. In the *Arthashastra*, what is the revenue from crown agricultural lands called?
    a) Janak
    b) Karna
    c) Sita
    d) Bali

9. With an approximate value of over ₹200 million, what was transferred to the treasury of the British East India Company in Lahore after the subjugation of Punjab in 1849?
   a) Kohinoor Diamond
   b) Peacock Throne
   c) The Sword of Tipu Sultan
   d) The Golden Throne of Maharaja Ranjit Singh

10. Which iconic brand identity was created by Eustace Fernandes in 1966?
    a) Air India's Maharaja
    b) Nirma's Dancing Girl
    c) Lijjat's Bunny
    d) Amul Girl

11. Which animal is the logo of Make in India, a manufacturing promotion campaign by the Government of India?
    a) Lion
    b) Tiger
    c) Elephant
    d) Horse

12. During whose reign was the finance minister called Amatya, a member of the Ashta Pradhan?
    a) Sher Shah Suri
    b) Ashoka
    c) Shivaji
    d) Chandra Gupta Maurya

13. The first recorded strike in India was organized by which group of workers in Calcutta in 1827?
    a) Railway coolies
    b) Sepoys
    c) Pankha pullers
    d) Palanquin bearers

14. Who called Sir Stafford Cripps' proposal a 'post-dated cheque on a failing bank'?
    a) Jawaharlal Nehru
    b) Muhammad Ali Jinnah
    c) Subhas Chandra Bose
    d) Mahatma Gandhi

15. In 1952, Godrej manufactured over 16 lakh units of what at the cost of ₹5 each?
    a) Bank lockers
    b) Ballot boxes
    c) Train door locks
    d) Car gears

16. The name of which airline is taken from a Sanskrit word that means 'limitless expanse'?
    a) Pawan Hans
    b) Zoom
    c) Pinnacle
    d) Vistara

17. Who, along with Mahbub ul Haq, developed the Human Development Index (HDI), which is used to rank countries into 4 tiers of human development?
    a) Manmohan Singh
    b) Jagdish Bhagwati

c) Amartya Sen
d) Montek Singh Ahluwalia

18. Who became the first male model for Lux in India in 2005?
    a) Aamir Khan
    b) Salman Khan
    c) Hrithik Roshan
    d) Shah Rukh Khan

19. Which motif appears on the reverse of the ₹2000 banknote that was rolled out in 2016?
    a) Mangalyaan
    b) Parliament Building
    c) Taj Mahal
    d) Peacock

20. 'It was only for the good of his subjects that he collected taxes from them, just as the sun draws moisture from the Earth to give it back a thousand fold'. In which book did Kalidasa write this, eulogizing the work of King Dalip?
    a) *Abhijñānaśākuntalam*
    b) *Meghdoot*
    c) *Vikramōrvaśīyam*
    d) *Raghuvaṃśa*

21. Which famous term was coined by Deepak Mohoni?
    a) Aadhaar
    b) Licence Raj
    c) Hindu rate of growth
    d) Sensex

22. The motifs on South Indian coins were confined to dynastic crests. What was the symbol used on Chola coins?
    a) Tiger
    b) Cat
    c) Peacock
    d) Snake

23. With which series of books would you associate Radhakrishnan Pillai?
    a) *Chanakya*
    b) *Chicken Soup for the Soul*
    c) *Dilbert Principle*
    d) *The One Minute Manager*

24. What started about 125 years back when a Parsi banker wanted to have home-cooked food regularly in office?
    a) Mavalli Tiffin Rooms
    b) Saravana Bhavan
    c) Mumbai Dabbawala
    d) Indian Railway Catering and Tourism Corporation

25. Cinnamon, Clove, Mustard, Chilli and Cardamom are different types of...
    a) Hotels by Oberoi Group
    b) SpiceJet planes
    c) Regional Headquarters of MDH Masala
    d) Newsletters by Spices Board India

CONNECTING INDIA

1. According to a list published by Google, who was the most searched Indian in 2016?
   a) Sonam Gupta
   b) Narendra Modi
   c) Salman Khan
   d) P.V. Sindhu

2. There are 9 PIN zones in India. The first 8 are geographical regions and the digit 9 is reserved for...
   a) Indian Army
   b) Indian Railways
   c) ISRO
   d) Parliament House

3. Malappuram was the first e-literate district in India. In which state is it located?
   a) Kerala
   b) Tamil Nadu
   c) Karnataka
   d) Andhra Pradesh

4. Who made the first mobile phone call in India to Sukh Ram in July 1995?
   a) A.P.J. Abdul Kalam
   b) Shankar Dayal Sharma
   c) P.V. Narasimha Rao
   d) Jyoti Basu

5. According to the 2014 Indian Readership survey results, which Hindi newspaper had the most number of readers?
   a) *Amar Ujala*
   b) *Navbharat Times*
   c) *Prabhat Khabar*
   d) *Dainik Jagran*

6. The last telegram was booked by Ashwani Mishra at the counter of Central Telegraph Office, Janpath, and the messages were sent to 2 people. One of them was S.M. Khan, the director general of DD news. Name the other person.
   a) Amitabh Bachchan
   b) Rahul Gandhi
   c) Sachin Tendulkar
   d) Mukesh Ambani

7. What is the STD code of New Delhi?
   a) 11
   b) 22
   c) 33
   d) 44

8. Whose portrait was depicted on the single-largest stamp issued in India on 20 August 1991?
   a) Lal Bahadur Shastri
   b) Ashoka
   c) Rajiv Gandhi
   d) M.S. Subbulakshmi

9. Which popular messenger application was founded

by Kavin Bharti Mittal?
a) Viber
b) Hike
c) WhatsApp
d) WeChat

10. Which of these works by Kalidasa shares its name with a type of postcard issued by India Post?
a) *Kumārasambhava*
b) *Meghdoot*
c) *Raghuvaṃśa*
d) *Ṛtusaṃhāra*

11. @mrsfunnybones is the Twitter handle of which famous celebrity?
a) Alia Bhatt
b) Deepika Padukone
c) Twinkle Khanna
d) Farah Khan

12. What is the name of the Quality Improvement Project undertaken by India Post to transform itself into a vibrant and responsive organization?
a) Project Glory
b) Project Arrow
c) Project Change
d) Project Dream Nation

13. Which organization gave the Indian government US$ 20,000 and 180 TV sets to start Doordarshan?
a) IMF
b) UNESCO

c) WHO
   d) UNICEF

14. Hikkim, located at an altitude of 14,567 feet, is the highest post office in India. In which state is it located?
    a) Uttarakhand
    b) Jammu and Kashmir
    c) Himachal Pradesh
    d) Sikkim

15. Who was the first newsreader on Doordarshan?
    a) Salma Sultan
    b) Pratima Puri
    c) Ramu Damodaran
    d) Prannoy Roy

16. In 1977, in which city was the first FM Channel launched by AIR on an experimental basis?
    a) Chennai
    b) Kolkata
    c) Delhi
    d) Mumbai

17. During his visit to India in 1959, which leader recorded an exclusive interview on AIR with K.P. Bhanumathy?
    a) Nelson Mandela
    b) Che Guevara
    c) Sun Yat-sen
    d) Fidel Castro

18. What is the motto of Doordarshan?
    a) Satyameva Jayate
    b) Satyam Shivam Sundaram
    c) Vande Mataram
    d) Mera Bharat Mahan

19. Which is the first privately owned Hindi satellite channel of India?
    a) Sony Entertainment
    b) Zee TV
    c) Star Plus
    d) MTV

20. Which weekly newspaper was started by Mahatma Gandhi in South Africa in 1903 that was initially issued in 4 languages?
    a) *Desh*
    b) *Bengal Gazette*
    c) *Indian Opinion*
    d) *Asiatic Mirror*

21. Complete the first tweet from the Twitter handle of Mangalyaan: 'What is red, is a planet and is the focus of my ____?'
    a) Search
    b) Orbit
    c) Path
    d) Mission

22. On which lake was India's first floating post office opened in 2011?
    a) Pushkar Lake

b) Dal Lake
c) Chilika Lake
d) Lake Pichola

23. Which 2008 film is based on a Chetan Bhagat novel about 6 friends working in a call centre whose lives change after a phone call from a special caller?
    a) *Tring Tring*
    b) *Kaun Hai*
    c) *Hello*
    d) *God Calling*

24. On 17 November 2014, Doordarshan was relaunched with a new theme and accompanied by a new punchline. Which of the following is the new punchline?
    a) Aapka Apna Channel
    b) Desh Ki Aawaz
    c) Desh Ka Apna Channel
    d) Desh Aagey Badhega

25. Which telecom operator launched commercial Internet services in India in August 1995?
    a) Vodafone
    b) BSNL
    c) VSNL
    d) Airtel

DRESSING UP

1. What are you wearing if you have put on Saleem Shahi?
   a) Footwear
   b) Jacket
   c) Headgear
   d) Belt

2. Pheran is the traditional dress of...
   a) Kerala
   b) Gujarat
   c) Kashmir
   d) Rajasthan

3. Which Oscar Award-winner designed costumes for *Gandhi, Lagaan: Once Upon a Time in India* and *Swades*?
   a) Aki Narula
   b) Rajeev Sethi
   c) Bhanu Athaiya
   d) Sandeep Khosla

4. Which of these saris is known to have traditional motifs and designs like bangadi-mor, kuyari, rui phool and asawali?
   a) Paithani
   b) Jamdani
   c) Kota
   d) Chanderi

5. On which part of the body is a nath worn?
   a) Hand
   b) Foot
   c) Ear
   d) Nose

6. Which state's traditional costume for women is called Lugade?
   a) Kerala
   b) Assam
   c) Maharashtra
   d) Bihar

7. In 1990, who made his debut as a costume designer in Bollywood with the film *Swarg*?
   a) Sandeep Khosla
   b) Sabyasachi Mukherjee
   c) Rohit Verma
   d) Manish Malhotra

8. Which of these is a dotted woven textile of Gujarat and is usually worn as a wrap-around skirt by the women of the Bharwad shepherd community?
   a) Tangaliya
   b) Korvai
   c) Ikat
   d) Shahtoosh

9. Which of these is a traditional headgear of Assam made of strips of bamboo and dried palm leaves, locally known as 'tokow-pat'?
   a) Japi

b) Parandi
c) Topor
d) Pheta

10. During Rongali Bihu, which of these garments are the women of Assam most likely to wear?
    a) Baku
    b) Mekhela Chador
    c) Lugade
    d) Mundum Neriyathum

11. Where are bangdi, naugari, bartana and dastband worn?
    a) Head
    b) Hand
    c) Foot
    d) Waist

12. Which city lends its name to full-length trousers worn for horse riding?
    a) Jodhpur
    b) Mumbai
    c) Bhopal
    d) Kolkata

13. The ancient korvai technique, which interlaces the borders with the body, is used to weave which sari?
    a) Paithani
    b) Chanderi
    c) Kanjeevaram
    d) Patola

14. Puanchei is a wrap-around skirt worn by the women of...
    a) Mizoram
    b) Madhya Pradesh
    c) Jammu and Kashmir
    d) Kerala

15. Who popularized the hip-length coat with a closed collar, which was once adopted by The Beatles?
    a) Bal Gangadhar Tilak
    b) Jawaharlal Nehru
    c) Rabindranath Tagore
    d) Rajendra Prasad

16. Which of these is a wedding sari that is gifted to Hindu and Jain brides in Gujarat by their maternal uncles?
    a) Kanjeevaram
    b) Paithani
    c) Panetar
    d) Chanderi

17. What is the art of body painting with a dye made from the leaves of Lawsonia inermis plant called?
    a) Kolam
    b) Mehndi
    c) Kalamkari
    d) Mandala

18. The men of which community in Sikkim wear a pagi made of striped cotton cloth?
    a) Mizo
    b) Khasi

c) Nepali
d) Lepcha

19. Which of these is used for eye make-up?
    a) Kohl
    b) Bhringaraj
    c) Parandi
    d) Kumkum

20. According to legend, which fabric was once gifted to Emperor Akbar in the hollow of a bamboo stick and when drawn out it was enough to cover an entire elephant?
    a) Chanderi
    b) Tussar
    c) Paithani
    d) Byomkai

21. The Kani shawl of Jammu and Kashmir has received the GI tag. What does 'Kani' mean?
    a) Thread
    b) Soft
    c) Wooden bobbins
    d) Colours

22. Who among these lent her name to a long, frock-style top worn by Madhubala in the song 'Jab Pyaar Kiya To Darna Kya'?
    a) Lakshmibai
    b) Padmavati
    c) Nur Jahan
    d) Anarkali

23. In the song 'Mera Joota Hai Japani' from the film *Shree 420*, the 'laal topi' was...
    a) Hindustani
    b) Roosi
    c) Cheeni
    d) Englishtani

24. Which silk is produced by the silkworm Antheraea assamensis?
    a) Eri
    b) Muga
    c) Tasar
    d) Mulberry

25. What is an achkan?
    a) A type of dhoti
    b) A sarong
    c) A knee-length coat
    d) A churidaar

ENABLING INDIA

1. In the 1960s, St. Mary Magdalene Church in Thumba in Thiruvananthapuram served as the main office of which of these?
   a) BSF
   b) NDA
   c) ISRO
   d) RBI

2. Which of these institutions started its journey in the old Hijli Detention Camp?
   a) IIT Kharagpur
   b) IIM Ahmedabad
   c) NID Ahmedabad
   d) NIT Silchar

3. Ranjana Sonawne became the first Indian to receive the Aadhaar card. She belongs to which village in Maharashtra that became India's first Aadhaar village?
   a) Chandrapur
   b) Jalgaon
   c) Belgaum
   d) Tembhli

4. The Reserve Bank of India acted as the Central Bank for which country till April 1947?
   a) Burma

b) Pakistan
   c) Bhutan
   d) Nepal

5. 'Hum Sab Bharatiya Hain, Hum Sab Bharatiya Hain, Apni Manzil Ek Hai, Ha, Ha, Ha, Ek Hai, Ho, Ho, Ho, Ek Hai. Hum Sab Bharatiya Hain.' This is the song of which organization in India?
   a) National Cadet Corps
   b) Sashastra Seema Bal
   c) Central Reserve Police Force
   d) Border Security Force

6. Which institution was established with the help of a generous grant from New Zealand under the Colombo Plan?
   a) All India Institute of Medical Sciences
   b) National Institute of Design
   c) Indian Statistical Institute
   d) Indian Institute of Management

7. After India became independent, K.M. Cariappa became the first commander-in-chief of the...
   a) Indian Army
   b) Indian Navy
   c) Indian Air Force
   d) Indian Coast Guard

8. Which colour forms the background of the flag of the Indian Air Force?
   a) Yellow
   b) Green

c) White
   d) Blue

9. The maritime zones of India are divided into 5 coast guard regions, namely, North-West, West, East, North-East and...
   a) Andaman and Nicobar
   b) Dadra and Nagar Haveli
   c) Puducherry
   d) Daman and Diu

10. What is the motto of the Border Security Force?
    a) Duty unto Death
    b) Unity and Discipline
    c) Service before Self
    d) Loyalty and Valour

11. Who served as the founder honorary director of IIM Ahmedabad from 1962 to 1965?
    a) C.V. Raman
    b) S. Radhakrishnan
    c) Vikram Sarabhai
    d) Amartya Sen

12. The acronym of RAF, the specialized wing of the CRPF, stands for _____ Action Force. Fill in the blank.
    a) Reliable
    b) Rapid
    c) Resurgent
    d) Radical

13. Which police force came into existence as the Crown Representative's Police on 27 July 1939?
    a) Central Reserve Police Force
    b) Border Security Force
    c) National Cadet Corps
    d) Sashastra Seema Bal

14. Which institution was founded on the basis of the recommendations made by Charles and Ray Eames to the Government of India in 1958?
    a) National Institute of Design
    b) Raman Research Institute
    c) Saha Institute of Nuclear Physics
    d) Netaji Subhas National Institute of Sports

15. In which city is the Indian Diamond Institute located?
    a) Surat
    b) Hyderabad
    c) Gwalior
    d) Ranchi

16. Which bird appears on the insignia of the National Defence Academy?
    a) Sparrow
    b) Dove
    c) Eagle
    d) Kingfisher

17. In whose honour was the Atomic Energy Establishment Trombay (AEET) renamed in 1966?
    a) Homi Jehangir Bhabha

b) J.C. Bose
c) Raja Ramanna
d) S.N. Bose

18. Which institution is housed in the erstwhile Palace of the Maharaja of Patiala?
    a) Netaji Subhas National Institute of Sports
    b) Birbal Sahni Institute of Palaeobotany
    c) Morarji Desai National Institute of Yoga
    d) Lakshmibai National University of Physical Education

19. Who was the first Indian to become the director of the Indian Institute of Science, Bengaluru?
    a) Meghnad Saha
    b) J.C. Bose
    c) C.V. Raman
    d) Vikram Sarabhai

20. The personnel of which organization are known as 'Himveers' or 'snow warriors'?
    a) Central Industrial Security Force
    b) Research and Analysis Wing
    c) Central Reserve Police Force
    d) Indo-Tibetan Border Police Force

21. Who was the first Indian to join the Indian Civil Service?
    a) Satyendranath Tagore
    b) Sukumar Sen
    c) R.D. Katari
    d) Subhas Chandra Bose

22. Established on 29 September 1688, the municipal corporation of which city is said to be the oldest municipal institution in India?
    a) Chennai
    b) Kolkata
    c) Mumbai
    d) Kochi

23. Who served as the president of the Film and Television Institute of India from 2002 to 2005?
    a) Shashi Kapoor
    b) Vinod Khanna
    c) Amol Palekar
    d) Dharmendra

24. In which city is the headquarters of the Lalit Kala Akademi located?
    a) Chennai
    b) Kolkata
    c) Mumbai
    d) New Delhi

25. By which name do we know the Delhi Special Police Establishement (DSPE) since 1 April 1963?
    a) NDA
    b) BSF
    c) NCC
    d) CBI

FULL TOSS

1. Who scored India's first Test century and was also the only bowler to dismiss Sir Don Bradman hit wicket?
   a) Vinoo Mankad
   b) Lala Amarnath
   c) Vijay Hazare
   d) Vijay Merchant

2. Which Indian cricketer's bat did Shahid Afridi use to score the fastest ODI century in 1996?
   a) Mohammad Azharuddin
   b) Ravi Shastri
   c) Sunil Gavaskar
   d) Sachin Tendulkar

3. Who are the only 2 Indian batsmen to bat on all 5 days of a Test match?
   a) Ravi Shastri and M.L. Jaisimha
   b) Sachin Tendulkar and Sourav Ganguly
   c) Rahul Dravid and V.V.S. Laxman
   d) Virender Sehwag and Gautam Gambhir

4. Who is the first Indian bowler to take a hat-trick in Test cricket?
   a) Kapil Dev
   b) Bishan Singh Bedi
   c) Anil Kumble
   d) Harbhajan Singh

5. Ashok Gandotra is the only cricketer who played for India but was born in…
   a) Chile
   b) Peru
   c) Argentia
   d) Brazil

6. He sang the romantic number 'Tu Mili Sab Mila' in the 2015 film *Meeruthiya Gangsters*. He has also played every single match that the IPL franchise Chennai Super Kings has ever played. Name the cricketer.
   a) M.S. Dhoni
   b) Ravichandran Ashwin
   c) Murali Vijay
   d) Suresh Raina

7. Who became the second bowler in the history of T20 cricket and the first in the history of IPL to take a 2-ball hat trick in 2014?
   a) Robin Uthappa
   b) Pravin Tambe
   c) Mohit Sharma
   d) Sandeep Sharma

8. Who gave Anil Kumble the nickname 'Jumbo' while playing an Irani Trophy match?
   a) Navjot Singh Sidhu
   b) Ravi Shastri
   c) Javagal Srinath
   d) Venkatesh Prasad

9. Which Indian cricketer represented Scotland in the National Cricket League in 2003?
   a) Sachin Tendulkar
   b) Rahul Dravid
   c) Saurav Ganguly
   d) Yuvraj Singh

10. Which Indian cricketer's autobiography is titled *The Test of My Life*?
    a) Sachin Tendulkar
    b) Saurav Ganguly
    c) Yuvraj Singh
    d) M.S. Dhoni

11. Playing 99 Test matches for his country, who is the only Indian to score 3 centuries in the first 3 Tests as well as another century in the last Test innings of his career?
    a) Rahul Dravid
    b) Mohammad Azharuddin
    c) Roger Binny
    d) Kapil Dev

12. Who is the first Indian cricketer to score a century on his ODI debut?
    a) Sarfaraz Khan
    b) K.L. Rahul
    c) Karun Nair
    d) Dhawal Kulkarni

13. Which Indian is famous for bowling the 'Sodukku Ball'?

a) Harbhajan Singh
   b) Ravichandran Ashwin
   c) Amit Mishra
   d) Ravindra Jadeja

14. About whom did Ian Chappell say: 'He can change the course of a match with the ease of Moses parting the Red Sea'?
    a) Suresh Raina
    b) M.S. Dhoni
    c) Virender Sehwag
    d) Yuvraj Singh

15. Which right-handed batsman, who made his international debut in a Twenty20 International against England at Manchester in August 2011, is a black belt in karate?
    a) Ajinkya Rahane
    b) Rohit Sharma
    c) Virat Kohli
    d) Ravindra Jadeja

16. Which city was the host to the first ever Indo-Pak Test match?
    a) Mumbai
    b) Bengaluru
    c) Kolkata
    d) New Delhi

17. Who was the first Indian batsman to score 10,000 runs in Test cricket?
    a) Sachin Tendulkar

b) Rahul Dravid
c) Sunil Gavaskar
d) Sourav Ganguly

18. Who is the first Indian to be dismissed for handling the ball in an ODI?
    a) Sunil Gavaskar
    b) Kapil Dev
    c) Vijay Hazare
    d) Mohinder Amarnath

19. In 2011, who became the first Indian to take a wicket off the 0th ball of his international T20 career?
    a) Virat Kohli
    b) Suresh Raina
    c) M.S. Dhoni
    d) Yuvraj Singh

20. Which Indian cricketer set a world record for the highest score by an individual in the second innings in ODIs when he scored an unbeaten 183 against Sri Lanka in 2005?
    a) Virender Sehwag
    b) M.S. Dhoni
    c) Sachin Tendulkar
    d) Yuvraj Singh

21. Who became the first blower to take a hat trick in the first over of an international Test match in 2006?
    a) Zaheer Khan
    b) Ajit Agarkar
    c) Irfan Pathan
    d) Anil Kumble

22. In 1964, who created a record of bowling 21 maiden overs in a row in a Test match against England in Madras?
    a) Salim Durani
    b) Subhash Gupte
    c) Polly Umrigar
    d) Bapu Nadkarni

23. In a Test match played in Kanpur against Australia in 1969, who became the first player to score a century and a duck on Test debut?
    a) B.S. Chandrasekhar
    b) Gundappa Viswanath
    c) S. Venkataraghavan
    d) Farokh Engineer

24. Before Virat Kohli, who was the only Indian to be dismissed hit wicket both in Tests and ODIs?
    a) Nayan Mongia
    b) Sunil Gavaskar
    c) Javagal Srinath
    d) Rahul Dravid

25. Who is the first Indian batsman to turn his maiden Test century into a triple century?
    a) Karun Nair
    b) Virender Sehwag
    c) Rohit Sharma
    d) K.L. Rahul

GOURMET

1. According to *Ain-i-Akbari*, what is made by freezing a mixture of khoa, nuts and kesar essence in conical metal receptacles after sealing it with dough?
   a) Rabri
   b) Firni
   c) Kulfi
   d) Barfi

2. What are Bhut Jolokia and Dhani types of?
   a) Hot chillies
   b) Rice
   c) Grapes
   d) Lentils

3. Which kebab shares its name with a small hamlet on the outskirts of Lucknow?
   a) Nehari
   b) Kakori
   c) Patili
   d) Nadroo

4. Bombay Duck is a type of…
   a) Duck
   b) Fish
   c) Potato
   d) Orange

5. Which of these gets its name from the Portuguese words for 'wine' and 'garlic'?
   a) Jalfrezi
   b) Vindaloo
   c) Do Pyaza
   d) Bhuna Gosht

6. It is called 'yang' in Kashmiri and 'ingu' in Kannada. What is its name in Hindi?
   a) Hing
   b) Saunf
   c) Kesar
   d) Dhania

7. Which of these is a Gujarati snack made mainly with gram flour and curd?
   a) Kachori
   b) Jalebi
   c) Khandvi
   d) Litti

8. Allahabad Safeda, Nagpur Seedless and Smooth Green are some of the varieties of which fruit?
   a) Guava
   b) Banana
   c) Mango
   d) Orange

9. Which of these is a steamed, sweet-flour dumpling stuffed with coconut and jaggery?
   a) Dhokla
   b) Modak

c) Firni
d) Appam

10. About which popular evening peasant meal did Jean-Baptiste Tavernier write that it was made of green gram, rice, butter and salt?
    a) Payasam
    b) Sambar
    c) Khichdi
    d) Appam

11. Which of these is a unique feature of Awadhi cuisine where the food is sealed in a large pan called handi and cooked on slow heat?
    a) Wazwan
    b) Dum Pukht
    c) Balchao
    d) Idiyappam

12. Which sweet is believed to have been invented in 1868 by confectioner Nobin Chandra Das in Kolkata?
    a) Rasgulla
    b) Barfi
    c) Malpua
    d) Lady Kenny

13. Thalipeeth is a traditional food item of which state in India?
    a) Maharashtra
    b) Kerala
    c) Odisha
    d) Bihar

14. Which of these is a Parsi dish usually made of vegetables and lentils?
    a) Litti
    b) Xacuti
    c) Dhansak
    d) Dhokla

15. Missi, Tandoori and Khoba are different varieties of which food item?
    a) Roti
    b) Dosa
    c) Pulao
    d) Kebab

16. Which of these is a GI-tagged product of Hyderabad?
    a) Hyderabadi Firni
    b) Kakori Kebab
    c) Byadgi Chilli
    d) Hyderabadi Haleem

17. Which of these spices is an excellent replacement for synthetic food colouring?
    a) Garlic
    b) Saffron
    c) Ginger
    d) Cardamom

18. Ambri is a variety of fruit that is indigenous to Kashmir. Name the fruit.
    a) Banana
    b) Grapes

c) Apple
d) Mango

19. Which of the following gets its name from Arabic words meaning 'Indian date'?
a) Plum
b) Cherry
c) Tamarind
d) Lemon

20. Which food was first introduced in Goa by the Portuguese and later became popular in Mumbai?
a) Pav
b) Bebinca
c) Kakori Kebab
d) Thepla

21. In Awadhi culture, what is a specialist in making naans, sheermals and kulchas called?
a) Wazwan
b) Nanfus
c) Bawarchi
d) Rakabdar

22. In Shahi Tukda, the 'Tukda' is...
a) A bowl of rice
b) A cube of sugar
c) A piece of cake
d) A slice of bread

23. The name of which of these dishes comes from a Gujarati word that means 'upside down'?

a) Undhiyu
b) Vindaloo
c) Aamti
d) Ragda

24. In 1670, which of these was first planted by Baba Budan with seeds brought from Yemen?
    a) Tea
    b) Coffee
    c) Cardamom
    d) Cashew

25. Which dish is said to have been invented by Kundan Lal Gujral?
    a) Doner Kebab
    b) Dal Makhani
    c) Vada Pav
    d) Masala Dosa

HOUSEFULL

1. Which film set a record by completing 700 weeks of continuous play in Mumbai's Maratha Mandir cinema in 2009?
   a) *Dil to Pagal Hai*
   b) *Lagaan*
   c) *Kuch Kuch Hota Hai*
   d) *Dilwale Dulhania Le Jayenge*

2. She has won the Miss World pageant. She was appointed the UNICEF Global Goodwill Ambassador in 2016. She released her debut single 'In My City' in 2012. Who is she?
   a) Aishwarya Rai Bachchan
   b) Sushmita Sen
   c) Priyanka Chopra
   d) Lara Dutta

3. The real-life meeting of which couple inspired the scene in which Rishi Kapoor meets Dimple Kapadia in her house in Bobby?
   a) Dilip Kumar and Saira Banu
   b) Rishi Kapoor and Neetu Singh
   c) Dharmendra and Hema Malini
   d) Raj Kapoor and Nargis

4. For which of these films did Sonam Kapoor charge only ₹11?
   a) *Delhi-6*

b) *Bhaag Milkha Bhaag*
c) *Aisha*
d) *Neerja*

5. *Romancing with Life* is the autobiography of which actor?
   a) Dev Anand
   b) Dilip Kumar
   c) Dharmendra
   d) Rishi Kapoor

6. Name the actor who played the role of a 12-year-old boy in a 2009 film and a 64-year-old chef in a 2007 film.
   a) Amitabh Bachchan
   b) Aamir Khan
   c) Dharmendra
   d) Vinod Khanna

7. What was Shah Rukh Khan's name in *Dil to Pagal Hai*, *Kuch Kuch Hota Hai*, *Kabhi Khushi Kabhie Gham* and *Chennai Express*?
   a) Raj
   b) Rahul
   c) Amit
   d) Arjun

8. Which of these films won in the Best Human Document category at the 1956 Cannes Film Festival?
   a) *Nirmalyam*
   b) *Pather Panchali*

c) *Mirza Ghalib*
   d) *Shyamchi Aai*

9. British Broadcasting Corporation (BBC) made a film titled *Bombay Superstar* in 1974. Whose life was it based on?
   a) Dilip Kumar
   b) Dev Anand
   c) Amitabh Bachchan
   d) Rajesh Khanna

10. Who portrayed the character of Shyam Sabu in the 1988 Hollywood film *Bloodstone*?
    a) Rajinikanth
    b) Kamal Hasaan
    c) Amitabh Bachchan
    d) Arvind Swamy

11. Which was the first Bollywood film to be produced by a Hollywood studio, Sony Pictures Entertainment?
    a) *Om Shanti Om*
    b) *Saawariya*
    c) *Jab We Met*
    d) *Chak De! India*

12. Which was the first full-length Hindi film to be shown at the United Nations?
    a) *Border*
    b) *Lage Raho Munna Bhai*
    c) *Swades*
    d) *Sholay*

13. What was the name of Yash Chopra's last film as a director?
    a) *Chandni*
    b) *Dil to Pagal Hai*
    c) *Veer Zaara*
    d) *Jab Tak Hai Jaan*

14. At the 1958 Academy Awards, the 5 nominees in the Best Foreign Film category were: *Nine Lives, Gates of Paris, The Devil Came at Night, The Nights of Cabiria* and...
    a) *Shri 420*
    b) *Mother India*
    c) *Neecha Nagar*
    d) *Jaagte Raho*

15. The autobiography of which film director is titled *An Unsuitable Boy*?
    a) Imtiaz Ali
    b) Karan Johar
    c) Sanjay Leela Bhansali
    d) Anurag Kashyap

16. Who was born as Mohammed Yusuf Khan in Peshawar?
    a) Dilip Kumar
    b) Raj Kapoor
    c) Dev Anand
    d) Dharmendra

17. The first full-length Indian feature film was based on the legend of...

a) Sant Tukaram
b) Raja Harishchandra
c) Sri Krishna
d) Alexander

18. Filmmaker Shekhar Kapur famously said: 'Indian film history can be divided into _____ BC and AD____'. Complete the quote.
    a) *Mughal-e-Azam*
    b) *Sholay*
    c) *Mother India*
    d) *Mera Naam Joker*

19. Released in 1931, which of these became the first Indian-talkie film?
    a) *Alam Ara*
    b) *Raja Harishchandra*
    c) *Shankuntala*
    d) *Lanka Dahan*

20. Which feature film on dairy issues was sponsored by 5,00,000 farmers of Gujarat?
    a) *Manthan*
    b) *Mandi*
    c) *Bazaar*
    d) *Arth*

21. Who made his directorial debut with the comedy film *Jaane Bhi Do Yaaro*?
    a) Satyajit Ray
    b) Mrinal Sen
    c) Shyam Benegal
    d) Kundan Shah

22. Who received the Dadasaheb Phalke Award in 1992?
    a) Bhupen Hazarika
    b) Manna Dey
    c) Bimal Roy
    d) Durga Khote

23. *My Dear Kuttichathan*, later dubbed in Hindi as *Chhota Chetan*, was the first...
    a) Indian film with two intervals
    b) 3D film
    c) Silent film in India
    d) Colour film in India

24. Who made his adult-film debut with Ketan Mehta's *Holi*?
    a) Shah Rukh Khan
    b) Saif Ali Khan
    c) Salman Khan
    d) Aamir Khan

25. Which actress was born as Begum Mumtaz Jehan Dehlavi?
    a) Meena Kumari
    b) Madhubala
    c) Waheeda Rehman
    d) Mumtaz

INCREDIBLE INDIA

1. In 1939, who became the vice chancellor of Banaras Hindu University?
   a) Madan Mohan Malaviya
   b) Dhondo Keshav Karve
   c) Bal Gangadhar Tilak
   d) S. Radhakrishnan

2. City of Joy Aid is a non-profit humanitarian organization founded by French author Dominique Lapierre. In which city is it based?
   a) Mumbai
   b) Kolkata
   c) Chennai
   d) Hyderabad

3. Who is referred to as Mokshadeva in Sanskrit?
   a) Hsūan Tsang
   b) Megasthenes
   c) Fa Hien
   d) Ibn Battuta

4. In which state is the Vechaar Utensils Museum located?
   a) Rajasthan
   b) Gujarat
   c) Tamil Nadu
   d) Odisha

5. According to the Mahabharata, what was the name of Gandhari's only daughter?
   a) Shanta
   b) Chitrangada
   c) Ulupi
   d) Dussala

6. Who served as a nominated member of the Rajya Sabha between 1986 and 1992?
   a) Shiv Kumar Sharma
   b) Hari Prasad Chaurasia
   c) Ravi Shankar
   d) M.S. Subbulakshmi

7. Which famous director directed *The River*, a film about 3 adolescent girls growing up in Bengal?
   a) Richard Attenborough
   b) Jean Renoir
   c) Federico Fellini
   d) Ingmar Bergman

8. Who was born in Almora on 13 May 1857, the year of the Sepoy Mutiny?
   a) E.M. Forster
   b) Ronald Ross
   c) Rudyard Kipling
   d) George Orwell

9. In 2015, Pravasi Bharatiya Divas marked 100 years of Mahatma Gandhi's return to India. In which city was it held?
   a) Gandhinagar

b) Champaran
   c) Gorakhpur
   d) Kolkata

10. Which cartoonist said: 'My sketch pen is not a sword, it's my friend'?
    a) R.K. Laxman
    b) R.K. Narayan
    c) M.F. Hussain
    d) Mahadevi Varma

11. Which was the first language to be officially accepted as a classical language of India?
    a) Sanskrit
    b) Kannada
    c) Tamil
    d) Odia

12. The earliest recorded reference of what can be traced to Lieutenant R. Wilcox's book *Memoir of a Survey of Assam and the Neighboring Countries*?
    a) Uranium
    b) Crude oil
    c) Diamond
    d) Tea

13. Which animal appears on the left side of the abacus on the national emblem of India?
    a) Bull
    b) Horse
    c) Lion
    d) Tiger

14. The Marathas gave the Portuguese a group of 72 villages as a mark of friendship. What is it now known as?
    a) Dadra and Nagar Haveli
    b) Daman and Diu
    c) Lakshadweep
    d) Puducherry

15. 'Bahujan Hitaya, Bahujan Sukhaya' is the motto of which organization?
    a) Reserve Bank of India
    b) India Post
    c) All India Radio
    d) Central Reserve Police Force

16. What is the colour of the cover of an Indian Diplomatic passport?
    a) Green
    b) White
    c) Blue
    d) Maroon

17. After Ganga, which river has the second largest basin covering 10 per cent of the area of India?
    a) Krishna
    b) Mahanadi
    c) Godavari
    d) Narmada

18. The foundation of which system of medicine, also practised in India, was laid by Hippocrates?
    a) Unani

b) Siddha
c) Homeopathy
d) Ayurveda

19. Bill Clinton once said: 'There are 2 kinds of people in the world. Those who have seen the ___ ___ and love it and those who have not seen the ___ ___ and love it.' Fill in the blanks.
    a) Taj Mahal
    b) Red Fort
    c) Gol Gumbaz
    d) Agra Fort

20. Who built the Adhai Din Ka Jhonpra in Ajmer?
    a) Ibrahim Lodi
    b) Sher Shah Suri
    c) Qutb ud-Din Aibak
    d) Shah Jahan

21. Which Nobel Prize winner's father was the first dean of Sir J.J. School of Art in Mumbai?
    a) Rudyard Kipling
    b) Rabindranath Tagore
    c) C.V. Raman
    d) Ronald Ross

22. If you were visiting the Sulabh International Museum of Toilets, which city would you be in?
    a) Chennai
    b) Kolkata
    c) Mumbai
    d) New Delhi

23. Who killed Dussashana in the war of Kurukshetra?
    a) Bhima
    b) Arjuna
    c) Nakula
    d) Sahadeva

24. In 1965, Philips pioneered the concept of Son et lumière shows in India. Where was the first show held?
    a) Taj Mahal
    b) Purana Qila
    c) Red Fort
    d) Victoria Memorial

25. Which prime minister of India shares his birthday with Mahatma Gandhi on 2 October?
    a) Lal Bahadur Shastri
    b) V.P. Singh
    c) Atal Bihari Vajpayee
    d) Morarji Desai

JUKEBOX

1. In whose honour was a street in Markham, Ontario, Canada, named in 2013?
   a) Zakir Hussain
   b) A.R. Rahman
   c) Ravi Shankar
   d) Ilayaraja

2. Who was the first musician to receive the Bharat Ratna?
   a) Ravi Shankar
   b) M.S. Subbulakshmi
   c) Zakir Hussain
   d) Shiv Kumar Sharma

3. Who was renamed after a famous character from her father's play Bhaaw Bandhan?
   a) Asha Bhosle
   b) Lata Mangeshkar
   c) Kavita Krishnamurthy
   d) Shreya Ghoshal

4. He was one of the participants on the singing reality show Fame Gurukul in 2005. Though he came sixth, he went on to become a famous playback singer in Bollywood. Name the singer.
   a) Arijit Singh
   b) Ankit Tiwari
   c) Mohit Chauhan
   d) Honey Singh

5. In 1948, after the assassination of Mahatma Gandhi, Husanlal Bhagatram, Rajendra Krishan and Mohammed Rafi created this song overnight following which Mohammed Rafi was invited by Jawaharlal Nehru to sing at his house. Name the song.
    a) 'Sabarmati Ke Sant Tune Kare Diya Kamal'
    b) 'Gun Dham Hamare Gandhiji'
    c) 'Sun Suno Aye Duniya Walon Bapu Ki Ye Amar Kahani'
    d) 'Vaishnav Jan To'

6. With which film did Shreya Ghoshal make her Bollywood debut as a playback singer?
    a) *Parineeta*
    b) *Devdas*
    c) *Jab We Met*
    d) *Kal Ho Naa Ho*

7. *How to Name It?*, *Nothing but Wind* and *Tiruvasagam: A Crossover* are non-film albums of…
    a) Ilayaraja
    b) O.P. Nayyar
    c) Naushad Ali
    d) Bhupen Hazarika

8. With which singer would you associate the defunct band Silk Route?
    a) Vishal Dadlani
    b) Sonu Nigam
    c) Shaan
    d) Mohit Chauhan

9. Who composed and recorded songs written by Atal Bihari Vajpayee in 2 albums, *Nayi Disha* and *Samvedna*?
   a) A.R. Rahman
   b) Shankar Mahadevan
   c) Jagjit Singh
   d) Pankaj Udhas

10. A.R. Rahman composed 'Ginga', an Oscar-nominated song, to celebrate the legacy of which sportsperson?
    a) Diego Maradona
    b) Muhammad Ali
    c) Pele
    d) Don Bradman

11. He started off as a software programmer but went on to become an established singer. He received the National Film Award, Best Male Playback Singer for the film *Taare Zameen Par*. Name the singer.
    a) Sonu Nigam
    b) Shankar Mahadevan
    c) Shaan
    d) Pritam

12. Which singer entered the *Guinness Book of World Records* in 2011 for the most number of single-studio recordings?
    a) Alka Yagnik
    b) Asha Bhosle
    c) Lata Mangeshkar

d) Sunidhi Chauhan

13. Surbahar is a larger version of which musical instrument?
    a) Dafli
    b) Bansuri
    c) Sitar
    d) Dhol

14. Who released the album *The Last Word* in Santoor in 2009?
    a) Zakir Hussain
    b) Bhimsen Joshi
    c) Amjad Ali Khan
    d) Shiv Kumar Sharma

15. Which semi-art music form was developed in Punjab by Shori Mian?
    a) Dhrupad
    b) Tappa
    c) Thumri
    d) Khayal

16. Who became the leader of the Tal Vadya Rhythm Band in 1973?
    a) Hariprasad Chaurasia
    b) Shiv Kumar Sharma
    c) Zakir Hussain
    d) Ravi Shankar

17. Which of these Padma Vibhushan awardees performed with his sons at the Nobel Peace Prize

Ceremony in Oslo, Norway, in 2014.
a) Shiv Kumar Sharma
b) Ravi Shankar
c) Bismillah Khan
d) Amjad Ali Khan

18. According to legend, what was created by splitting the pakhawaj into 2 parts?
a) Ghatam
b) Dholak
c) Tabla
d) Nagara

19. Who composed his first song for the film Funtoosh when he was just 9 years old?
a) R.D. Burman
b) Bappi Lahiri
c) S.D. Burman
d) Naushad

20. As a tribute to whom did Pandit Ravi Shankar compose a new raga and name it Mohankauns?
a) Mahatma Gandhi
b) Jawaharlal Nehru
c) Rabindranath Tagore
d) Subhas Chandra Bose

21. Which musician was so inspired by Indian music that he named his son Dhani, after the 2 notes in Indian classical music?
a) Eric Clapton
b) George Harrison

c) Bob Dylan
d) Mick Jagger

22. Who among these received the rare honour of being invited by the first Indian Prime Minister, Jawaharlal Nehru, to perform at the Red Fort in Delhi on 15 August 1947?
    a) Bismillah Khan
    b) Ravi Shankar
    c) Shiv Kumar Sharma
    d) Hariprasad Chaurasia

23. Who taught raga Megha Malhar to his daughter to perform in front of emperor Akbar?
    a) Kalidasa
    b) Tansen
    c) Purandara Dasa
    d) Baiju Bawra

24. Chaiti is a folk song of...
    a) Rajasthan
    b) Uttar Pradesh
    c) Odisha
    d) Kerala

25. As of 2017, who has won 8 Filmfare Awards, or the highest number of awards, for Best Playback Singer (Male)?
    a) Mukesh
    b) Kishore Kumar
    c) Manna Dey
    d) Mohammad Rafi

KNOW ALL

1. Which city was referred to as the 'Oxford of the East' by Pandit Jawaharlal Nehru?
   a) Benaras
   b) Pune
   c) Aligarh
   d) Jamshedpur

2. An illustrated manuscript of the *Tutinama* is said to be the first work of the...
   a) Pala School
   b) Mughal School
   c) Pahari School
   d) Deccani School

3. What is the name of the eldest daughter of Samuel Richmond Noble, who became a teacher at an early age and taught at different schools in Ireland and England before moving to India?
   a) The Mother of Pondicherry
   b) Sister Nivedita
   c) Mother Teresa
   d) Annie Besant

4. Which famous poet and author wrote Urdu poems under the pen name Rasa?
   a) Bharatendu Harishchandra
   b) Munshi Premchand

c) Mahadevi Varma
   d) Maithilisharan Gupt

5. Who laid the foundation stone of Chhatrapati Shivaji Maharaj Vastu Sangrahalaya?
   a) Queen Victoria
   b) King George V
   c) Mahatma Gandhi
   d) Pherozeshah Mehta

6. Which tree appears on the logo of the Reserve Bank of India?
   a) Neem
   b) Coconut
   c) Palm
   d) Mango

7. What was the original name of the Mahabharata composed by Vyasa?
   a) Meera
   b) Tara
   c) Jaya
   d) Maya

8. In which state is Panna, a place known for its diamond mines, located?
   a) Madhya Pradesh
   b) Andhra Pradesh
   c) Odisha
   d) Bihar

9. Who directed a documentary on his teacher Benode

Behari Mukherjee titled *The Inner Eye*?
a) Satyajit Ray
b) Mrinal Sen
c) Manjit Bawa
d) M.F. Hussain

10. Who was the first chairman of the University Grants Commission (UGC)?
    a) P.C. Mahalanobis
    b) Shanti Swarup Bhatnagar
    c) Birbal Sahni
    d) J.C. Bose

11. Which state has the highest population according to the 2011 census?
    a) Uttar Pradesh
    b) Bihar
    c) Maharashtra
    d) Tamil Nadu

12. Who started sharing his thoughts with the people of India on a programme titled Mann Ki Baat, every month from 3 October 2014?
    a) Narendra Modi
    b) Pranab Mukherjee
    c) Baba Ramdev
    d) A.P.J. Abdul Kalam

13. What did D. Udaya Kumar design by combining the Devanagari letter Ra and Roman letter R?
    a) Mascot of the Royal Challengers Bangalore
    b) The logo of RAF

c) The Supreme Court of India
d) The rupee symbol

14. The length of the international border of which state is 856 kilometres, about 84 per cent of its total border?
    a) Bihar
    b) Tripura
    c) Punjab
    d) Rajasthan

15. Who served as the minister of Railways and Transport in the Central Cabinet from 1951 to 1956?
    a) Lal Bahadur Shastri
    b) Charan Singh
    c) B.R. Ambedkar
    d) Lala Lajpat Rai

16. In 1952, who was appointed as the chairman of the Calendar Reform Committee?
    a) Meghnad Saha
    b) J.C. Bose
    c) U.N. Brahmachari
    d) C.V. Raman

17. Who among these leaders is also known as Mahamana?
    a) Madan Mohan Malaviya
    b) Lala Lajpat Rai
    c) Bipin Chandra Pal
    d) B.R. Ambedkar

18. Siddha system is one of the oldest systems of medicine in India. In which of the following languages is Siddha literature written?
    a) Tamil
    b) Telugu
    c) Marathi
    d) Odia

19. Operation Flood, launched in 1970 by the National Dairy Development Board, was the brainchild of...
    a) V. Kurien
    b) M.S. Swaminathan
    c) Vandana Shiva
    d) Baba Amte

20. Which Indian city did Le Corbusier design by using the structure of the human body?
    a) Gandhinagar
    b) Chandigarh
    c) Jamshedpur
    d) Kochi

21. In which state is Rani Ki Vav (the Queen's Stepwell) located?
    a) Gujarat
    b) Rajasthan
    c) Maharashtra
    d) Tamil Nadu

22. Who was born as Eric Arthur Blair in Motihari, Bihar, in the year 1903?
    a) George Orwell

b) E.M. Forster
   c) William Dalrymple
   d) Gerald Durrel

23. Who is considered as the father of the Indian space programme?
    a) Meghnad Saha
    b) C.V. Raman
    c) Homi Jehangir Bhabha
    d) Vikram Sarabhai

24. Who cursed Sri Krishna that he would be killed by trickery?
    a) Madri
    b) Draupadi
    c) Gandhari
    d) Kunti

25. For centuries which dance form was performed only by the Nattuvans of Tanjore district?
    a) Kathak
    b) Bharatanatyam
    c) Kuchipudi
    d) Sattriya

LANDSCAPE

1. Which Indian state has the longest coastline?
   a) Tamil Nadu
   b) Gujarat
   c) Andhra Pradesh
   d) Karnataka

2. The Ranchi Plateau is the largest division of which of these plateaus?
   a) Deccan
   b) Malwa
   c) Kolar
   d) Chhota Nagpur

3. Which country does the Radcliffe Line separate India from?
   a) Bangladesh
   b) Nepal
   c) Bhutan
   d) Pakistan

4. Which river has Gomti and Ghagra as its tributaries?
   a) Mahanadi
   b) Godavari
   c) Kaveri
   d) Ganga

5. Which of the following separates Little Andaman from the Nicobar Islands?
   a) Zero Mile River
   b) Ten Degree Channel
   c) Hundred Furlong Canal
   d) Thousand Yard Bridge

6. What name is given to the broad coastal plain in eastern Tamil Nadu?
   a) Malabar Coast
   b) Kathiawar coast
   c) Coromandel Coast
   d) Konkan coast

7. In 1907, where did the British install a sandstone obelisk called the Zero Mile Stone, marking the approximate centre of India?
   a) Allahabad
   b) Nagpur
   c) Varanasi
   d) Indore

8. What is black cotton soil called in India?
   a) Usar
   b) Regur
   c) Bhangar
   d) Khadar

9. On which island would you find the only active volcano in India?
   a) Barren Island
   b) Dead Island

c) Desolate Island
d) Sterile Island

10. The Siliguri Corridor—a narrow strip of land that connects the Indian mainland with the outlying border states of the Northeast—is also know as the Eastern...
    a) Duck's Neck
    b) Chicken's Neck
    c) Sparrow's Neck
    d) Turkey's Neck

11. Bitra is the smallest inhabited island of which union territory?
    a) Dadra and Nagar Haveli
    b) Daman and Diu
    c) Lakshadweep
    d) Puducherry

12. Within which mountain range does the Siachen glacier lie?
    a) Satpura
    b) Vindhya
    c) Aravalli
    d) Karakoram

13. Which waterfall in India is also known as Gautamdhara?
    a) Jog
    b) Jonha
    c) Dudhsagar
    d) Arvalem

14. Which lake has 4 main interconnected basins: Gagribal, Hazratbal, Bod dal and Nagin?
    a) Dal Lake
    b) Chilika Lake
    c) Pulicat Lake
    d) Hussain Sagar Lake

15. Which state is bordered by Nagaland in the north, Assam in the west, Mizoram in the southwest and Myanmar in the south and east?
    a) Manipur
    b) Tripura
    c) Sikkim
    d) Odisha

16. The Thar Desert covers about 61 per cent of the total landmass of...
    a) Haryana
    b) Rajasthan
    c) Madhya Pradesh
    d) Punjab

17. Which mountain was first climbed from its Nepal side in 1953 by British mountaineer Charles Evans?
    a) Doddabetta
    b) Nanda Devi
    c) Mount Everest
    d) Kangchenjunga

18. In which state of India would you find the wettest place on Earth?
    a) Nagaland

b) Mizoram
c) Manipur
d) Meghalaya

19. Which lake was formed when a meteor crashed into the Earth at an estimated speed of 90,000 kmph?
    a) Chilika Lake
    b) Dal Lake
    c) Lonar Lake
    d) Lake Pichola

20. Which state in India was the largest producer of raw jute from 2015–2016?
    a) Andhra Pradesh
    b) Assam
    c) West Bengal
    d) Bihar

21. According to *Guinness Book of World Records*, which is the world's largest river island?
    a) Majuli
    b) Sriharikota
    c) Diu
    d) Munroe

22. Which of these is often referred to as 'the second-coldest inhabited place in the world'?
    a) Drass
    b) Tawang
    c) Pelling
    d) Keylong

23. Nubra Valley, one of the highest deserts in the world, is located in which state of India?
    a) Nagaland
    b) Jammu and Kashmir
    c) Himachal Pradesh
    d) Assam

24. Which is the highest point in Tamil Nadu?
    a) Dodabetta
    b) Guru Shikhar
    c) Anamudi
    d) Reo Purgyil

25. Which river was known as Hyphasis in Greek and Vipasha in Sanskrit?
    a) Chenab
    b) Sutlej
    c) Beas
    d) Ravi

MIXED BAG

1. Who suggested the title of R.K. Narayan's novel *Swami and Friends*?
   a) Graham Greene
   b) W.B. Yeats
   c) William Faulkner
   d) E.M. Forster

2. Who served as the first president of the Asiatic Society?
   a) Charles Wilkins
   b) William Jones
   c) Jonathan Duncan
   d) Nathaniel Brassey Halhed

3. What did Shri Bhanubhai Shah donate to Amdavad Municipal Corporation that led to the inauguration of a very different kind of museum on 27 February 1986?
   a) Kites
   b) Utensils
   c) Shoes
   d) Books

4. Who was the first Sultan of Delhi?
   a) Khizr Khan
   b) Qutb ud-Din Aibak
   c) Alauddin Khilji
   d) Muhammad bin Tughluq

5. Famous for its miniature paintings, in which state is Mewar located?
   a) Maharashtra
   b) Madhya Pradesh
   c) Gujarat
   d) Rajasthan

6. The name of which tree comes from a word for Hindu merchants who conducted their business under this tree?
   a) Pipal
   b) Banyan
   c) Neem
   d) Teak

7. What is the town of Pampore in Jammu and Kashmir famous for?
   a) Glass bangles
   b) Saffron
   c) Oranges
   d) Coffee

8. Who discovered Urea Stibamine, an organic antimonial compound that played an important part in the treatment of Kala-azar?
   a) J.C. Bose
   b) U.N. Brahmachari
   c) C.V. Raman
   d) Ronald Ross

9. 12 November is celebrated as Public Service Broadcasting Day to commemorate…

a) The renaming of AIR as Akashwani
b) Gandhiji's visit to AIR
c) The opening of its 100th station
d) Guglielmo Marconi's birthday

10. Who began his career as a cartoonist for the newspaper *Milap* with his comic strip 'Daabu'?
    a) K. Shankar Pillai
    b) Pran
    c) R.K. Laxman
    d) Abu Abraham

11. What among these was first commercially mined in 1774 by Sumner and Heatly of East India Company in Raniganj along the Western bank of river Damodar?
    a) Coal
    b) Uranium
    c) Diamond
    d) Gold

12. Which dance form derives its textual sanction from *Balarama Bharatam* and *Hastalakshana Deepika*?
    a) Kathakali
    b) Mohiniyattam
    c) Manipuri
    d) Odissi

13. How many spokes does the Ashoka Chakra in the Indian national flag have?
    a) 20
    b) 22

c) 24
d) 26

14. Fill in the blank to complete this quote by Mother Teresa: 'Peace begins with a _____.'
    a) Smile
    b) Handshake
    c) Kind word
    d) Wink

15. Which sage is believed to have created Kurukshetra?
    a) Parashurama
    b) Vishrava
    c) Agastya
    d) Durvasa

16. Who was the court poet of Ala ud-Din Khilji?
    a) Amir Khusrau
    b) Abul Fazl
    c) Faizi
    d) Mirza Ghalib

17. What is the state tree of Maharashtra?
    a) Palmyra
    b) Mango
    c) Coconut
    d) Sal

18. In which language was the song 'Vande Mataram' composed?
    a) Bengali
    b) Sanskrit

c) Hindi
d) Pali

19. On the main entrance of which iconic building in New Delhi would you find Ram Kinkar Baij's sculptures of Yaksha and Yakshini?
    a) Reserve Bank of India
    b) All India Radio
    c) Border Security Force
    d) Supreme Court of India

20. Which monument was commissioned by Nawab Asaf-ud-Daula of Lucknow as a famine relief measure?
    a) Bara Imambara
    b) Charminar
    c) Gol Gumbaz
    d) Hawa Mahal

21. Which state of India is famous for the Kalighat paintings?
    a) Tamil Nadu
    b) Bihar
    c) Maharshtra
    d) West Bengal

22. Whose story does *Gita Govinda* narrate?
    a) Rama and Sita
    b) Malavika and Agnimitra
    c) Radha and Krishna
    d) Arjun and Draupadi

23. Which is the first month of the year according to the National Calendar of India?
    a) Chaitra
    b) Magha
    c) Phalguna
    d) Pausha

24. On which author's novels are the films *Rudaali* and *Hazaar Chaurasi Ki Maa* based?
    a) Kamala Das
    b) Ashapoorna Devi
    c) Mahadevi Varma
    d) Mahasweta Devi

25. In India, the Golden Triangle in tourism is formed by Jaipur, New Delhi and...
    a) Agra
    b) Gwalior
    c) Gaya
    d) Nainital

NEXT-DOOR NEIGHBOURS

1. Which of these countries is not one of the founding members of South Asian Association for Regional Cooperation (SAARC)?
   a) Sri Lanka
   b) Bangladesh
   c) Maldives
   d) Afghanistan

2. Ananda Samarakoon, who studied at Shantiniketan in India, went on to create the national anthem of which country?
   a) Nepal
   b) Sri Lanka
   c) Bhutan
   d) Vietnam

3. Which river originates in the Kailash ranges of Himalayas, just south of the Konggyu Tsho Lake, at an elevation of 5150 metres?
   a) Brahmaputra
   b) Indus
   c) Irrawaddy
   d) Ganga

4. Whose sacred tooth does The Temple of the Tooth Relic in Sri Lanka contain?
   a) Ashoka

b) Mahavira
   c) Buddha
   d) Raja Raja Chola

5. With which country does the Maitree Express connect India?
   a) Bangladesh
   b) Pakistan
   c) Nepal
   d) Bhutan

6. The Salma Dam is also known as the _____ India Friendship Dam. Fill in the blank.
   a) Bangla
   b) Sino
   c) Nepal
   d) Afghan

7. Who passed away the day after he signed the Tashkent Agreement—an accord to end the August–September 1965 war between India and Pakistan?
   a) Lal Bahadur Shastri
   b) Jawaharlal Nehru
   c) Gulzarilal Nanda
   d) Morarji Desai

8. Who wrote the story *Kabuliwala* about a Pathan merchant from Kabul and a 5-year-old girl Mini?
   a) Premchand
   b) Rabindranath Tagore
   c) Amrita Pritam
   d) R.K. Narayan

9. After whom is the highest national recognition for outstanding achievements in the field of adventure on land, sea and air named?
   a) Tenzing Norgay
   b) Narain Karthikeyan
   c) Jim Corbett
   d) Kalpana Chawla

10. With which country does India share its longest international border?
    a) Nepal
    b) Bangladesh
    c) Pakistan
    d) China

11. Which foreign dignitary studied political science at Lady Shri Ram College in New Delhi and graduated in 1964?
    a) Sheikh Hasina
    b) Aung San Suu Kyi
    c) Benazir Bhutto
    d) Yingluck Shinawatra

12. With which movie did the Pakistani actress Mahira Khan make her Bollywood debut?
    a) *Raees*
    b) *Kaabil*
    c) *Rangoon*
    d) *Phillauri*

13. Which famous actress was crowned Miss Universe Sri Lanka in 2006?

a) Jacqueline Fernandez
   b) Katrina Kaif
   c) Nargis Fakhri
   d) Freida Pinto

14. To which Indian cricketer did former Pakistani President Pervez Musharraf say: 'A lot of placards in the crowd have suggested that you should get a haircut. But if you take my advice, you look good in this hairstyle'?
    a) Sachin Tendulkar
    b) Sourav Ganguly
    c) M.S. Dhoni
    d) Yuvraj Singh

15. In 1952, who was the captain of Pakistan's first Test match against India after the team had gained Test status?
    a) Israr Ali
    b) Nazar Mohammad
    c) Abdul Hafeez Kardar
    d) Hanif Mohammad

16. Who wrote the *Śrīmad Bhagavadgītā Rahasya*, while serving a 6-year-prison sentence in the Mandalay jail?
    a) Bal Gangadhar Tilak
    b) Lala Lajpat Rai
    c) Bipin Chandra Pal
    d) Subhas Chandra Bose

17. Mano Majra, a fictional village on the border of Pakistan and India, forms the backdrop of which famous book?

a) *Train to Pakistan*
   b) *Toba Tek Singh*
   c) *Freedom at Midnight*
   d) *Midnight's Children*

18. The Buddhist monk Sehi travelled to India in 402 CE and initiated Sino-Indian relations. How do we know him better?
    a) Hiuen Tsiang
    b) Fa Hien
    c) Megasthenes
    d) Marco Polo

19. About three-fifths of the total area of the Sundarbans is in...
    a) Nepal
    b) Bangladesh
    c) Bhutan
    d) Sri Lanka

20. Who married the famous Pakistani cricketer Shoaib Malik in 2010?
    a) Dia Mirza
    b) Sania Mirza
    c) Katrina Kaif
    d) Huma Qureshi

21. According to a 2011 report, Bhojpuri is spoken by 5.3 per cent of the people in which country?
    a) Sri Lanka
    b) Maldives
    c) Mauritius
    d) Bangladesh

22. Apart from Nelson Mandela, who is the only non-Indian to have received the Bharat Ratna?
    a) Sirimavo Bandaranaike
    b) Sheikh Mujibur Rahman
    c) Aung San Suu Kyi
    d) Khan Abdul Ghaffar Khan

23. In 2015, which country received the largest share of Indian foreign aid?
    a) Nepal
    b) Bhutan
    c) Sri Lanka
    d) Bangladesh

24. His grandfather was the chief guest during the 1954 Republic Day celebrations in India. His father was the chief guest in 1984 and 2005. He himself was the chief guest in 2013. Who are we talking about?
    a) George W. Bush
    b) Norodom Sihamoni
    c) Jigme Khesar Namgyel Wangchuck
    d) Anura Bandaranaike

25. After 1948, which language on the language panel of a 10 rupee note was substituted with Oriya?
    a) Dzongkha
    b) Nepali
    c) Urdu
    d) Burmese

OUTSTANDING PERFORMANCES

1. Hungarian–Russian Eve Yvonne Maday de Maros, who later came to be known as Savitri Bai, is famous for...
   a) Returning the Bharat Ratna Award
   b) Being the first woman recipient of Ashok Chakra
   c) Receiving the Jnanpith Award thrice
   d) Designing the Param Vir Chakra medal

2. On which day are the Bravery Awards announced?
   a) 26 January
   b) 5 September
   c) 2 October
   d) 14 November

3. The Padma Vibhushan Award was instituted in 1954. It had three classes, namely, Pahela Varg, Dusra Varg and Tisra Varg. In 1955, what was Dusra Varg renamed as?
   a) Padma Vibhushan
   b) Padma Bhushan
   c) Padma Shri
   d) Bharat Ratna

4. Which sportsperson received the Arjuna Award in 1999, the Rajiv Gandhi Khel Ratna Award in 2001, the Padma Shri in 2005, the Dronacharya Award in 2009 and the Padma Bhushan in 2014?

a) Pullela Gopichand
   b) Sachin Tendulkar
   c) Prakash Padukone
   d) Mahesh Bhupathi

5. Which organization received the Gandhi Peace Prize in 2014?
   a) Indian Railways
   b) Prasar Bharati
   c) ISRO
   d) Grameen Bank

6. Which of these awards is given 'to honour eminent coaches who have successfully trained sportspersons or teams and enabled them to achieve outstanding results in international competitions'?
   a) Arjuna Award
   b) Dronacharya Award
   c) Bhishma Award
   d) Vishwamitra Award

7. Which of these awards, instituted in 1961, were offshoots of the Ashoka Chakra series of gallantry awards?
   a) Bharat Ratna
   b) Seva medals
   c) Jeevan Raksha Padak Awards
   d) Padma Awards

8. The Filmfare Awards were initially named after the editor of a newspaper. What was the name of these awards?

a) Mrinal
b) Shireen Awards
c) Clare Awards
d) Akbar Awards

9. In what language must a literary work be in order to be eligible for Vyas Samman Award?
a) Sanskrit
b) Hindi
c) Marathi
d) Telugu

10. Ashok Chakra Awards are biannual and are given on 26 January and...
a) 12 March
b) 2 October
c) 15 August
d) 25 December

11. Who was the first woman to receive the Jnanpith Award?
a) Amrita Pritam
b) Ashapurna Devi
c) Kamala Surayya
d) Mahasweta Devi

12. Which of these is the name of the award that is given in honour of the founder director of the Council of Scientific and Industrial Research?
a) Har Gobind Khorana Award
b) Shanti Swarup Bhatnagar Prize
c) A.P.J. Abdul Kalam Award

d) Dr Vikram Sarabhai Prize

13. For contribution in which field does the government of Madhya Pradesh confers the Kumar Gandharva Award?
    a) Urdu poetry
    b) Music
    c) Weaving
    d) Film direction

14. The 2009 Rajiv Gandhi Khel Ratna Award had 3 recepients, 2 of whom belonged to same field of sports. Name that sport.
    a) Boxing
    b) Cricket
    c) Tennis
    d) Athletics

15. For which book did its author win the first ever Sahitya Akademi Award in English language?
    a) *The Guide*
    b) *Fire on the Mountain*
    c) *Shadow from Ladakh*
    d) *Scholar Extraordinary*

16. Three peacetime gallantry awards are given away on 26 January. They are Ashok Chakra, Kirti Chakra and...
    a) Aditya Chakra
    b) Shaurya Chakra
    c) Maha Vir Chakra
    d) Arjun Chakra

17. Which of these awards is not given by the Ministry of Youth Affairs and Sports in India?
    a) Maulana Abul Kalam Azad Trophy
    b) Eklavya Awards
    c) Arjuna Awards
    d) Dronacharya Awards

18. Which was the film that won the first Filmfare Award in the Best Film category in 1954?
    a) *Baiju Bawra*
    b) *Do Bigha Zamin*
    c) *Daag*
    d) *Devdas*

19. Dadasaheb Phalke Award is given for contribution to...
    a) Hindi literature
    b) Indian cinema
    c) Indigenous sports
    d) Environment protection

20. Who is the first sportsperson to have received the Bharat Ratna?
    a) Kapil Dev
    b) Sachin Tendulkar
    c) P.T. Usha
    d) Viswanathan Anand

21. The government of which state established the Dr Vikram Sarabhai Award in 1995–1996 to promote and encourage research and developmental activities?
    a) Rajasthan

b) Kerala
   c) Maharashtra
   d) Gujarat

22. If the Golden Lotus Award is called Swarna Kamal, by what name do we also know the Silver Lotus Award?
    a) Peetal Kamal
    b) Rajat Kamal
    c) Loh Kamal
    d) Tamra Kamal

23. The Bharat Ratna is shaped like the leaf of which tree?
    a) Peepal
    b) Banyan
    c) Gulmohar
    d) Coconut

24. The Maithilisharan Gupt Award is given to honour excellence in the field of...
    a) Essays in Hindi
    b) Urdu poetry
    c) English literature
    d) Hindi poetry

25. Which is the peacetime equivalent of the Param Vir Chakra?
    a) Shaurya Chakra
    b) Vir Chakra
    c) Kirti Chakra
    d) Ashok Chakra

PLAY OFF

1. Which Indian holds the record for winning the most number of mixed doubles titles in the Open Era?
   a) Leander Paes
   b) Mahesh Bhupathi
   c) Rohan Bopanna
   d) Somdev Devvarman

2. The former name of which Indian city is common with a trophy in rugby contested for annually between England and Scotland?
   a) Bombay
   b) Madras
   c) Bangalore
   d) Calcutta

3. Which team co-owned by Sahara India Pariwar and M.S. Dhoni in the Hockey India League replaced the defunct Ranchi Rhinos?
   a) Ranchi Riders
   b) Ranchi Rockers
   c) Ranchi Rays
   d) Ranchi Roosters

4. Sakshi Malik, the first Indian Olympic medal winner at Rio Olympics 2016, was an employee of which of the following organizations during her achievement?
   a) Indian Railways
   b) State Bank of India

c) Indian Police Service
d) Indian Army

5. The 2014 film Badlapur Boys is based on which traditional sport of India?
   a) Kabaddi
   b) Kho Kho
   c) Malla-Yuddha
   d) Pehlwani

6. Who among these won the Arjuna Award for kabaddi in 2015?
   a) Anup Kumar
   b) Rakesh Kumar
   c) Manjeet Chillar
   d) Ajay Thakur

7. Who among the following won a gold medal in wrestling at the 2014 Incheon Asian Games?
   a) Yogeshwar Dutt
   b) Sushil Kumar
   c) Ravinder Singh
   d) Palwinder Singh Cheema

8. Badminton is derived from which ancient sport played by the British officers in India?
   a) Gillidanda
   b) Kancha
   c) Poona
   d) Bandy

9. In 1932, which team became the first Indian men's

sports team to do an around-the-world tour?
a) Indian Hockey Team
b) Indian Football Team
c) Indian Cricket Team
d) Indian Kabaddi Team

10. In 2012, which Padma Bhushan awardee became the third Indian woman after Karnam Malleswari and Saina Nehwal to win an Olympic medal?
a) Deepika Kumari
b) Sania Mirza
c) Geeta Phogat
d) Mary Kom

11. Who is first Indian woman to reach the final of an Olympic event?
a) P.T. Usha
b) Karnam Malleswari
c) Dipa Karmakar
d) P.V. Sindhu

12. In 2016, in which event did Deepa Malik participate to become the first Indian woman to win a Paralympics medal?
a) Swimming
b) Shooting
c) Shot Put
d) Archery

13. In 2002, which Indian became the first to win a gold medal in boxing in the Commonwealth Games?
a) Vijender Singh

b) Mary Kom
   c) Mohammed Ali Qamar
   d) Shiva Thapa

14. In 2013, which Indian player ended his contract with Portuguese club Sporting Lisbon's reserve team and signed with JSW Sports?
    a) Bhaichung Bhutia
    b) Robin Singh
    c) Sunil Chhetri
    d) Subrata Pal

15. Which Indian archer was ranked No. 1 in 2012 when she was competing in the World Cup individual stage in Turkey?
    a) Dola Banerjee
    b) Deepika Kumari
    c) Bombayala Devi
    d) Chekrovolu Swuro

16. Yubi Lakpi is the Manipuri version of which sport?
    a) Cricket
    b) Volleyball
    c) Basketball
    d) Rugby

17. In 2014, which sportsperson from India was appointed as the United Nations Women's Goodwill Ambassador for South Asia?
    a) Saina Nehwal
    b) Geeta Phogat
    c) Sania Mirza
    d) Mary Kom

18. Which sport is known as Hu-Tu-Tu in some parts of western India and Ha-Do-Do in some parts of eastern India ?
    a) Kho Kho
    b) Kabaddi
    c) Mallkhamb
    d) Kalaripayattu

19. Who did Ashwini Ponnappa team up with to win a silver medal at the 2014 Commonwealth Games?
    a) Jwala Gutta
    b) Saina Nehwal
    c) P.V. Sindhu
    d) Prajakta Sawant

20. In 2006, who became the first Indian woman and the youngest player from Asia to win a 4-star tournament in badminton?
    a) Ashwini Ponnappa
    b) P.V. Sindhu
    c) Saina Nehwal
    d) Chetan Anand

21. Who is the first Indian sportsperson to be bestowed with the Padma Vibhushan, the second-highest civilian award in India?
    a) Sunil Gavaskar
    b) Bhaichung Bhutia
    c) Viswanathan Anand
    d) Yogeshwar Dutt

22. Who became the first Indian to win the men's singles

title at the prestigious All England Championships and was declared World No. 1 in 1980?
a) Syed Modi
b) Prakash Padukone
c) Nandu M. Natekar
d) U. Vimal Kumar

23. Which is the first domestic football club from India to not only wear boots but also to hire a professional trainer?
a) Mohun Bagan
b) Dempo
c) East Bengal
d) Mohammedan Sporting

24. It is often believed that the people of Vienna paid a tribute to this sportsperson by erecting his statue and giving it 4 hands and 4 sticks to signify his amazing control over the ball. Who was this person?
a) Dhyan Chand
b) Leslie Claudius
c) Gurbux Singh
d) K.D. Singh

25. Which of the following sports was made a state sport by Madhya Pradesh in 2013?
a) Kushti
b) Mallakhamb
c) Kho Kho
d) Kabaddi

QUILL PEN

1. Who composed the Telugu epic poem *Amuktamalyada*?
   a) Krishnadevaraya
   b) Chandragupta Maurya
   c) Harshavardhana
   d) Raja Raja Chola

2. In which Amitav Ghosh book would you meet Kesri Singh, Zachary Reid and Shireen Modi?
   a) *The Hungry Tide*
   b) *Flood of Fire*
   c) *The Shadow Lines*
   d) *The Circle of Reason*

3. The first stanza of which poem published in *Tattvabodhini Patrika* in 1911 became our National Anthem?
   a) *Vande Mataram*
   b) *Matribhumi*
   c) *Bharat Vidhata*
   d) *To India*

4. In the introduction to which book did W.B. Yeats write: 'The work of a supreme culture, they yet appear as much the growth of the common soil as the grass and the rushes.'?
   a) *Guide*

b) *Gitanjali*
c) *Fruit Gathering*
d) *Coolie*

5. The Arabic translation of which literary work is known as *Kalīlah wa Dimnah*, named after the 2 jackals that figure in the first story?
   a) *Mudrarakshasa*
   b) *Bhagavad Gita*
   c) *Panchatantra*
   d) *Manusmriti*

6. With which language is the ancient sangam literature associated?
   a) Sanskrit
   b) Tamil
   c) Bengali
   d) Malayalam

7. Who wrote a major part of *India Divided* while he was still in prison?
   a) Rajendra Prasad
   b) Mahatma Gandhi
   c) Jawaharlal Nehru
   d) Subhas Chandra Bose

8. Who called India 'the sovereign empress of the past' and stopped writing poetry after the Jallianwala Bagh massacre?
   a) Kamala Das
   b) Sarojini Naidu
   c) Aurobindo Ghosh
   d) Rabindranath Tagore

9. How do we better know the famous Urdu poet Raghupati Sahay?
   a) Munshi Premchand
   b) Tota-e-Hind
   c) Gulzar
   d) Firaq Gorakhpuri

10. 'Andheri Raat Mein Deepak Jalaye Kaun Baitha Hai' is the first line of which poem by Harivansh Rai Bachchan?
    a) *Parichay*
    b) *Makan*
    c) *Arya*
    d) *Jugnu*

11. Which author's autobiography is titled *Truth, Love and a Little Malice*?
    a) Khushwant Singh
    b) Durjoy Datta
    c) V.S. Naipaul
    d) Ruskin Bond

12. Whose first story appeared in the magazine *Zamana* published from Kanpur?
    a) Munshi Premchand
    b) Rabindranath Tagore
    c) Harivansh Rai Bachchan
    d) Bankim Chandra Chatterjee

13. Who was the first woman to receive the Sahitya Akademi Award?
    a) Mahadevi Varma

b) Mahasweta Devi
c) Amrita Pritam
d) Sarojini Naidu

14. Whose well-known work *Swadeshi Samaj* was published in 1904?
    a) Mahatma Gandhi
    b) Rabindranath Tagore
    c) Munshi Premchand
    d) Bal Gangadhar Tilak

15. Amish Tripathi's book *Scion of Ikshvaku* is based on the life of...
    a) Shiva
    b) Rama
    c) Krishna
    d) Brahma

16. Who is the author of *Beastly Tales from Here and There* (1992), which consists of 10 stories about animals told in verse?
    a) Amish Tripathi
    b) Chetan Bhagat
    c) Vikram Seth
    d) Kiran Desai

17. Which of these occupies chapters 23 to 40 of Book VI of the Mahabharata?
    a) *Bhagavad Gita*
    b) *Rig Veda*
    c) *Matsya Purana*
    d) *Raghuvaṃśa*

18. *Ateet Ke Chalachitra* is a collection of short stories based on whose interactions with women during her stint as a principal of a school for girls?
    a) Sarojini Naidu
    b) Mahadevi Varma
    c) Kamala Das
    d) Ismat Chughtai

19. Which of these is the earliest epic poem in Tamil written by Prince Ilanko Adikal?
    a) *Silappatikaram*
    b) *Raghuvaṃśa*
    c) *Tirukkural*
    d) *Meghdoot*

20. Who wrote *Ghashiram Kotwal*, recognized as one of the longest-running plays in the world?
    a) Vijay Tendulkar
    b) Mahesh Dattani
    c) Bhisham Sahni
    d) Habib Tanvir

21. Which lyrical poem by Kalidasa inspired Friedrich Schiller's play *Maria Stuart*?
    a) *Gita Govinda*
    b) *Meghdoot*
    c) *Raghuvaṃśa*
    d) *Kumārasambhava*

22. With which film did Chetan Bhagat make his Bollywood debut as a screenplay writer?
    a) *Kick*

b) *Dabangg 2*
c) *Sultan*
d) *Dhoom 3*

23. Who wrote a foreword to the novel *Untouchable* by Mulk Raj Anand?
    a) E.M. Forster
    b) Saki
    c) W.B. Yeats
    d) Graham Greene

24. Complete the name of a novel by R.K. Narayan. *Waiting for the _____*.
    a) *Mahatma*
    b) *Lokmanya*
    c) *Netaji*
    d) *Sardar*

25. Our national song 'Vande Mataram' is a poem in which novel?
    a) *Godaan*
    b) *Anandamath*
    c) *Antima Aranya*
    d) *Gora*

REMARKABLE WOMEN

1. Chhavi Rajawat, a management graduate, became the first woman sarpanch of Soda village. In which state is Soda located?
   a) Rajasthan
   b) Arunachal Pradesh
   c) Gujarat
   d) Sikkim

2. Born in Euclid, Ohio, she became the second woman of Indian origin to go into space. Name her.
   a) Kalpana Chawla
   b) Sunita Williams
   c) Shawna Pandya
   d) Anousheh Ansari

3. In 2014, who teamed up with Joshna Chinappa to clinch gold in the women's doubles final at the Commonwealth Games?
   a) Sakshi Malik
   b) Sania Mirza
   c) Saina Nehwal
   d) Dipika Pallikal

4. She has had an illustrious career of over 50 years. She has sung for the likes of Nargis and Preity Zinta. She is nicknamed 'The Nightingale of Bollywood'. Who is she?

a) M.S. Subbulakshmi
   b) Shamshad Begum
   c) Lata Mangeshkar
   d) Asha Bhosle

5. Reita Faria was the first Indian to...
   a) Be crowned Miss World
   b) Cross the English Channel
   c) Win the Pulitzer Prize
   d) Win an Olympic bronze

6. Who published her first volume of poetry in 1905 titled *The Golden Threshold*, which was followed by her second title in 1912, *The Bird of Time*?
   a) Kamala Surayya
   b) Sarojini Naidu
   c) Amrita Pritam
   d) Mahadevi Varma

7. After Shah Jahan ascended the throne in 1628, Nur Jahan was exiled to which city to live in seclusion and spend the last days of her life?
   a) Shahjahanabad
   b) Fatehpur Sikri
   c) Agra
   d) Lahore

8. Who was the first recipient of the Dadasaheb Phalke Award?
   a) Durga Khote
   b) Devika Rani
   c) Surayya
   d) Meena Kumari

9. Who succeeded Rukn ud-Din Firuz on the throne of Delhi?
   a) Nur Jahan
   b) Razia Sultan
   c) Chand Bibi
   d) Mumtaz Mahal

10. Who is the first Indian woman cricketer to get the prestigious life membership of the Marylebone Cricket Club?
    a) Jhulan Goswami
    b) Mithali Raj
    c) Anjum Chopra
    d) Anju Jain

11. A lady named Mirra Alfassa played an integral part in establishing the township of Auroville. How do we know her better?
    a) Sister Nivedita
    b) The Mother
    c) Mother Teresa
    d) Annie Besant

12. Who said: 'Being a woman by itself is a gift of God which all of us must appreciate. The origin of a child is a mother, and is a woman. A woman is the one who shares love and shows a man what sharing, caring and loving is all about. That is the essence of a woman.'?
    a) Aishwarya Rai
    b) Priyanka Chopra

c) Lara Dutta
d) Sushmita Sen

13. The chairman and CEO of PepsiCo, Indra Nooyi, was born in which city of India?
    a) Chennai
    b) Hyderabad
    c) Bengaluru
    d) Mumbai

14. Famously known as Rani of Jhansi, Lakshmibai was born into a Maratha Brahmin family and was named _____.
    a) Mehr al-Nesa
    b) Meera
    c) Manikarnika
    d) Sita Devi

15. Who became the first Indian woman to hold a cabinet portfolio in 1937?
    a) Vijaya Lakshmi Pandit
    b) Indira Gandhi
    c) Sarojini Naidu
    d) Aruna Asaf Ali

16. In 2000, for which book did Jhumpa Lahiri win the Pulitzer Prize in Fiction?
    a) *Interpreter of Maladies*
    b) *The Namesake*
    c) *Unaccustomed Earth*
    d) *One World: A Global Anthology of Short Stories*

17. Cornershop, the British-indie rock band, paid tribute to Asha Bhosle in a song titled...
    a) 'Brimful of Asha'
    b) 'Heartful of Asha'
    c) 'Soulful of Asha'
    d) 'Breathful of Asha'

18. Who became the first woman to be appointed as the United Nations Civilian Police Adviser in the Department of Peacekeeping Operations in 2003?
    a) Kiran Bedi
    b) Punita Arora
    c) Puja Thakur
    d) Priya Jayakumar

19. She has been a member of the Prime Minister's Council on Trade and Industry of India. In 2011, she was conferred with the Padma Bhushan. She is the managing director and chief executive officer of India's largest private sector bank. Name her.
    a) Padmasree Warrior
    b) Chanda Kochhar
    c) Alka Banerjee
    d) Indra Nooyi

20. Who is the first Indian to win the World Junior Badminton Championship and the Super Series tournament?
    a) P.V. Sindhu
    b) Ashwini Ponnappa
    c) Jwala Gutta
    d) Saina Nehwal

21. From 2015 to 2017, which Indian actor starred as Alex Parrish in the American television series *Quantico*?
    a) Deepika Padukone
    b) Sonam Kapoor
    c) Priyanka Chopra
    d) Alia Bhatt

22. Who said: 'The person who gives with a smile is the best giver because God loves a cheerful giver.'?
    a) Sister Nivedita
    b) Mirra Alfassa
    c) Annie Besant
    d) Mother Teresa

23. Who was the first woman to receive the Bharat Ratna?
    a) Mother Teresa
    b) Indira Gandhi
    c) Sushmita Sen
    d) Annie Besant

24. Written with Santha Rama Rau, *A Princess Remembers* is the autobiography of which queen from India?
    a) Princess Niloufer Farhat Begum Saheba of Hyderabad
    b) Sita Devi of Kapurthala
    c) Indira Raje of Baroda
    d) Maharani Gayatri Devi of Jaipur

25. In 1990, who was listed in the *Guinness Book of World Records* for her achievement as the first Indian woman mountaineer to climb Mount Everest?
    a) Bachendri Pal
    b) Premlata Agarwal
    c) Santosh Yadav
    d) Dicky Dolma

STATE OF THE ART

1. Taipchi, Jali, Zanzeera and Khatau are some of the stiches used in which type of embroidery?
   a) Chikankari
   b) Phulkari
   c) Katha
   d) Kasuti

2. In the Gandhara art form, whose had wavy hair, wore robes like the Roman toga and resembled the Greek Apollo?
   a) Buddha
   b) Ganesha
   c) Mahavira
   d) Ravana

3. Coloured glass base embossed with golden miniature artwork is the special attraction of…
   a) Bidri work
   b) Thewa artwork
   c) Pithora Art
   d) Warli Art

4. The Channapatna taluk is famous for which of these things made of a special wood known as 'aale mara'?
   a) Clay pottery
   b) Toys
   c) Jewellery
   d) Wood panels

5. Traditionally, in which of these styles of paintings is gold leaf and precious and semi-precious stones liberally used?
   a) Tanjore
   b) Kalamkari
   c) Madhubani
   d) Warli

6. During whose reign was *Hamzanama*, a series of 1,400 paintings on cloth, created?
   a) Akbar
   b) Jahangir
   c) Shah Jahan
   d) Aurangzeb

7. What are gota patti, kantha, kasuti and sujani different types of?
   a) Metal casting
   b) Embroidery
   c) Textile printing
   d) Bags

8. The bidriware is a GI-tagged handicraft of which state of India?
   a) Karnataka
   b) West Bengal
   c) Madhya Pradesh
   d) Kerala

9. Unique to Rajasthan, Bagru, Sanganer and Barmeri are techniques of...
   a) Textile printing

b) Kite making
c) Tying turbans
d) Footwear making

10. The Blue Boy, Blacksmith, and Santhal Dance are some of the works of which artist?
    a) Jamini Roy
    b) Nandalal Bose
    c) Jatin Das
    d) Ram Kinkar Baij

11. Cave 10 of which UNESCO World Heritage site has fragments of the oldest-surviving painting of the life of the Buddha and an image of his first sermon at Sarnath?
    a) Ajanta caves
    b) Ellora caves
    c) Bhimbetka caves
    d) Elephanta caves

12. In Kashmir, the unique art of making ceiling by fitting small pieces of wood is called...
    a) Kettuvallam
    b) Dhokra work
    c) Shibori
    d) Khatamband

13. After the birth of his first son, who quit painting cinema hoardings and began working at the Fantasy Furniture Shop, Mumbai, as a furniture and toy designer?
    a) M.F. Husain

b) Satish Gujral
c) Ram Kinkar Baij
d) Tyeb Mehta

14. Which technique gets its name from a Malay-Indonesian word meaning 'tied' or 'bound'?
a) Phulkari
b) Ikat
c) Bandhini
d) Shibori

15. Since the seventeenth century, artisans from the Viswakarma community are involved in the making of which GI-tagged musical instrument?
a) Surbahar
b) Thanjavur Veena
c) Udukkai
d) Swarmandal

16. Which place is associated with the applique work that is used on the canopy of the 3 chariots used during Rath Yatra at Puri?
a) Tinsukia
b) Pipli
c) Guwahati
d) Rajkot

17. Who used waste products like broken crockery, bicycle frames, bottles, glass bangles, cooking pots, etc. to create the Rock Garden of Chandigarh?
a) Satish Gujral
b) Nek Chand

c) Sudarsan Pattnaik
d) Ram Kinkar Baij

18. The Kishangarh-style of miniature painting depicts whom as Radha and Krishna?
    a) Raja Sawant Singh and Bani Thani
    b) Bajirao and Mastani
    c) Prithviraj and Sanyogita
    d) Bimbisara and Amrapali

19. About whom did R.K. Laxman write: 'The bespectacled ____ ____ in his checked coat had walked into my cartoon spontaneously, as if I had no hand in his creation'?
    a) Ordinary Person
    b) Common Man
    c) Public Figure
    d) Aam Janta

20. Pomacha, laharia and chunari are different styles of...
    a) Tying and dyeing
    b) Carpet weaving
    c) Applique work
    d) Phulkari stitching

21. Who had won the Governor's Gold Medal in 1873 for the painting *Nair Lady Adorning Her Hair*?
    a) Jamini Roy
    b) Raja Ravi Varma
    c) Nandalal Bose
    d) Amrita Shergill

22. Warli painting is a GI-registered handicraft of which state?
    a) Assam
    b) Tamil Nadu
    c) Bihar
    d) Maharashtra

23. Which of these involves the decoration of gold with intricate enamelwork?
    a) Phulkari
    b) Chikankari
    c) Minakari
    d) Kalamkari

24. Which of these is an ancient Rajasthani art form?
    a) Phad painting
    b) Madhubani painting
    c) Kalighat Pattachitra
    d) Warli painting

25. Fill in the blank to complete this statement by Mahatma Gandhi: '_____ women are born weavers, they weave fairy tales in their cloth.'
    a) Punjabi
    b) Rajasthani
    c) Assamese
    d) Marathi

TAKE OFF

1. In which Indian city was an open double-decker tour bus named Nilambari introduced?
   a) Mumbai
   b) New Delhi
   c) Bengaluru
   d) Chennai

2. What is the colour of the cover of the official passport in India?
   a) Maroon
   b) Navy blue
   c) White
   d) Dark green

3. The coaches of which train are named after regions of Maharashtra?
   a) Palace on Wheels
   b) Deccan Odyssey
   c) Golden Chariot
   d) Southern Splendour

4. In January 1941, who escaped his ancestral house in a car bearing the number plate BLA 7169?
   a) Subhas Chandra Bose
   b) Bhagat Singh
   c) Mahatma Gandhi
   d) Veer Savarkar

5. The name of which of these is derived from a Tamil word that literally means 'tied wood'?
   a) Kayak
   b) Dhow
   c) Shikara
   d) Catamaran

6. How many digits would you find in the PNR number of a railway ticket?
   a) 9
   b) 10
   c) 12
   d) 13

7. What did the British colonialists use as hotels in Kashmir after foreigners were prohibited from purchasing land to build resorts?
   a) Caravans
   b) Houseboats
   c) Train coaches
   d) Bus terminals

8. Inspired by Jules Verne's classic tale *Around the World in 80 Days*, Monisha Rajesh travelled around India and wrote a book about her adventures titled *Around India in 80* _____.
   a) *Trains*
   b) *Buses*
   c) *Planes*
   d) *Autorickshaws*

9. In which city was the first electric bus launched in India in 2014?
   a) Mumbai
   b) Chennai
   c) Bengaluru
   d) Kolkata

10. In 1971, Air India took delivery of its first Boeing 747 and named it after…
    a) Mahavira
    b) Ashoka
    c) Jawaharlal Nehru
    d) Mahatma Gandhi

11. What kind of animal is Bholu, the official mascot of Indian Railways?
    a) Tiger
    b) Elephant
    c) Giraffe
    d) Rhinoceros

12. In which of these films does Meenakshi, a Hindu-Brahmin woman, protect a Muslim man during a bus journey?
    a) *Taxi No. 9211*
    b) *Mr and Mrs Iyer*
    c) *The Darjeeling Limited*
    d) *Yeh Jawaani Hai Deewani*

13. Which novel revolves around Adela Quested and Mrs Moore's travels to India?
    a) *Bhindi Bazar*

b) *A Passage to India*
c) *Kim*
d) *Bhowani Junction*

14. Initially created and designed by Bobby Kooka and Umesh Rao for memo-pads, who adopted the Maharajah as their mascot in 1946?
a) Indian Railways
b) Air India
c) Shipping Corporation of India
d) National Highways Authority of India

15. If NH stands for National Highway and SH stands for State Highway, what does MDR stand for?
a) Main District Road
b) Major District Road
c) Main District Route
d) Minor District Road

16. Which 1971 film, starring Asha Parekh and Jeetendra, is named after a vehicle equipped for living in?
a) *Tonga*
b) *Caravan*
c) *Houseboat*
d) *Shikara*

17. After whom is the Raipur airport named?
a) B.R. Ambedkar
b) Swami Vivekananda
c) Jawaharlal Nehru
d) Sarojini Naidu

18. In 1998, what was certified by the *Guinness Book of World Records* as the world's oldest steam locomotive in regular operation?
    a) Deccan Odyssey
    b) The Kohinoor
    c) Blue Orient
    d) Fairy Queen

19. Who wrote the poem *Palanquin Bearers*?
    a) Sarojini Naidu
    b) Jawaharlal Nehru
    c) Harivansh Rai Bachchan
    d) Nissim Ezekiel

20. After which famous person is the Port Blair airport named?
    a) Rajiv Gandhi
    b) Subhas Chandra Bose
    c) Veer Savarkar
    d) Sarojini Naidu

21. In Mumbai if you were travelling by a 'Victoria', what would it be?
    a) Bus
    b) Horse carriage
    c) Rickshaw
    d) Steamer

22. After whose work is the Godan Express named?
    a) Munshi Premchand
    b) Rabindranath Tagore
    c) Harivansh Rai Bachchan

d) Mulk Raj Anand

23. In which city did the first tram run from Sealdah to Armenian Ghat?
    a) Kolkata
    b) Mumbai
    c) Chennai
    d) New Delhi

24. Which of the following railway stations was known as Victoria Terminus Station?
    a) Kalka Shimla Railway
    b) New Delhi Railway Station
    c) Chhatrapati Shivaji Maharaj Terminus
    d) Howrah Junction Railway Station

25. Which state capital does the famous Kempegowda International Airport serve?
    a) Bengaluru
    b) Patna
    c) Shimla
    d) Itanagar

UNITY IN DIVERSITY

1. Which festival involves a procession led by shehnai players and dancers carrying large floral fans to Yogmaya Temple and the dargah of Khwaja Bakhtiyar Kaki in Mehrauli?
   a) Sindhu Darshan Festival
   b) Phool Waalon Ki Sair
   c) Ashadhi Ekadashi
   d) Gangasagar Mela

2. In which festival do people tie a piece of cloth, some sugar crystals, a garland, a few neem and mango leaves to the tip of a bamboo pole and hoist it outside their houses?
   a) Pongal
   b) Gudi Padwa
   c) Nowruz
   d) Poila Boishakh

3. In which Northeastern state is the Hornbill Festival held?
   a) Assam
   b) Nagaland
   c) Manipur
   d) Mizoram

4. During Durga Puja, traditionally on which day does the 'sindur khela' take place?

a) Ashtami
   b) Saptami
   c) Navami
   d) Dashami

5. In India, the Sonepur fair is said to be the largest...
   a) Crafts fair
   b) Cattle fair
   c) Bird fair
   d) Book fair

6. Eid ul-Fitr literally means the 'festival of _____'.
   a) Rekindling hope
   b) Putting an end to miseries
   c) Breaking the fast
   d) Lights

7. In which state is the Nagaur Fair held every year in February?
   a) West Bengal
   b) Rajasthan
   c) Maharashtra
   d) Gujarat

8. Whose 350th birth anniversary was celebrated in Patna in January 2017?
   a) Mahavira
   b) Guru Gobind Singh
   c) Buddha
   d) Chaitanya Mahaprabhu

9. Which of the following commemorates the day Jesus Christ was crucified?
   a) Christmas
   b) Good Friday
   c) All Souls Day
   d) Thanksgiving Day

10. With which of these festivals would you associate the Sunder Mundriye folklore?
    a) Rongali Bihu
    b) Gudi Padwa
    c) Lohri
    d) Ugadi

12. Pongal is an important festival of Tamil Nadu. What does the word 'pongal' mean?
    a) Pot of rice
    b) To boil
    c) Happiness
    d) Colours

13. In which month is Makar Sankranti celebrated?
    a) January
    b) February
    c) March
    d) April

14. In which state is the Tarnetar fair held?
    a) Uttarakhand
    b) West Bengal
    c) Rajasthan
    d) Gujarat

15. Where is Hemis Festival celebrated?
    a) Mussoorie
    b) Ladakh
    c) Shillong
    d) Kasauli

16. The Puri Rath Yatra takes place near which of these temples?
    a) Meenakshi Amman Temple
    b) Jagannath Temple
    c) Brihadeeswarar Temple
    d) Mahabodhi Temple

17. Which of these videos by Coldplay shows the celebration of Holi?
    a) *Princess of China*
    b) *Hymn for the Weekend*
    c) *Charlie Brown*
    d) *Fix You*

18. With which festival would you associate the mission: 'To preserve and refurbish the heritage arts district of Mumbai with the cooperation of local authorities'?
    a) Surajkund Mela
    b) Kala Ghoda Arts Festival
    c) Modhera Dance Festival
    d) Toshali Craft Fair

19. In which city of Rajasthan is the Kolayat Fair held?
    a) Bikaner
    b) Kota

c) Ajmer
d) Jaisalmer

20. Bihu, an important festival of Assam, is divided into 3 categories: Maagh, Kaati and…
    a) Simui
    b) Diwara
    c) Morani
    d) Bohag

21. Which of these takes place in Haryana during the first fortnight of each February?
    a) Ganga Mahotsav
    b) Surajkund International Crafts Mela
    c) Masi Magam
    d) Pushkar Fair

22. The Mahamastakabhisheka is an important Jain festival held once every 12 years in the town of Shravanabelagola. In this festival, the statue of Lord Gomateshwara is bathed in milk, saffron, turmeric, etc. In which state is Shravanabelagola located?
    a) Tamil Nadu
    b) Karnataka
    c) Kerala
    d) Odisha

23. Kumbh Mela is held in 4 places: Prayag, Haridwar, Ujjain and…
    a) Bhopal
    b) Indore
    c) Nashik
    d) Surat

24. Eid ul-Fitr marks the end of the month-long fast of Ramadan and the beginning of which Islamic month?
    a) Rajab
    b) Shawwal
    c) Safar
    d) Rabiul-Awwal

25. Whose birth anniversary is celebrated as Vesak in India?
    a) Mahavira
    b) Buddha
    c) Guru Nanak
    d) Ramakrishna Paramhansa

VOICES

1. Fill in the blank to complete this quote by Albert Einstein: 'We owe a lot to the Indians, who taught us how to _____, without which no worthwhile scientific discovery could have been made.'
   a) Write
   b) Count
   c) Draw
   d) Analyse

2. Who said: 'Bombs and pistols do not make a revolution. The sword of revolution is sharpened on the whetting-stone of ideas'?
   a) Mother Teresa
   b) Mahatma Gandhi
   c) Vikram Sarabhai
   d) Bhagat Singh

3. Who said these words: 'If I were asked under what sky the human mind has most fully developed some of its choicest gifts, has most deeply pondered on the greatest problems of life, and has found solutions, I should point to India.'
   a) Max Mueller
   b) Lord Clive
   c) Karl Marx
   d) Queen Victoria

4. Fill in the blank to complete this quote by Mahatma Gandhi: 'I claim that in losing the _____ we lost our left lung.'
   a) Great leader G.K. Gokhale
   b) Spinning wheel
   c) Concept of cleanliness
   d) Battle

5. Whose words are these: 'An American economist has predicted that in the next century India will be an economic superpower. I do not want India to be an economic superpower. I want India to be a happy country.'?
   a) Mahatma Gandhi
   b) Atal Bihari Vajpayee
   c) Mother Teresa
   d) J.R.D. Tata

6. Whose most famous speech ended with the words: 'And to India, our much-loved motherland, the ancient, the eternal and the ever-new, we pay our reverent homage and we bind ourselves afresh to her service. Jai Hind.'?
   a) Subhas Chandra Bose
   b) Swami Vivekananda
   c) Jawaharlal Nehru
   d) Mahatma Gandhi

7. In a famous book, who wrote: 'I recollect it was settled by general consent that India was quite a misrepresented country, and had nothing

objectionable in it, but a tiger or two, and a little heat in the warm part of the day.'?
a) Charles Dickens
b) William Faulkner
c) Jonathan Swift
d) Daniel Defoe

8. According to Shah Rukh Khan, '_____ is not a good teacher, _____ makes you humble.'
a) Success, failure
b) Happiness, grief
c) Hope, despair
d) Deceit, honesty

9. Who said: 'Every blow aimed at me is a nail in the coffin of British imperialism'?
a) Maulana Abul Kalam Azad
b) Lala Lajpat Rai
c) B.R. Ambedkar
d) Lal Bahadur Shastri

10. Whose said the following: 'If there is one place on the face of Earth where all the dreams of living men have found a home from the very earliest days when man began the dream of existence, it is India.'?
a) Max Mueller
b) Romain Rolland
c) Jean-Paul Sartre
d) Bertrand Russell

11. In 1893, in which city did Swami Vivekananda give his famous speech starting with the words:

'Sisters and Brothers of America'?
a) Houston
b) Boston
c) Los Angeles
d) Chicago

12. Who said: 'I've made seventeen or eighteen films now, only two of which have been original screenplays, all the others have been based on short stories or novels, and I find the long short story ideal for adaptation.'?
a) Raj Kapoor
b) Satyajit Ray
c) Govind Nihalani
d) Shyam Benegal

13. Who gave the famous: 'Give me blood, and I shall give you freedom' speech in Burma in 1944?
a) Bal Gangadhar Tilak
b) Vallabhbhai Patel
c) Bipin Chandra Pal
d) Subhas Chandra Bose

14. According to A.P.J. Abdul Kalam, what is a continuous process and not an accident?
a) Excellence
b) Prosperity
c) Happiness
d) Growth

15. Who said: 'Earth provides enough to satisfy every man's need, but not every man's greed'?

a) Mahatma Gandhi
b) A.P.J. Abdul Kalam
c) S. Radhakrishnan
d) Rabindranath Tagore

16. Fill in the blank to complete this quote by C.V. Raman: 'I am the master of my failure... If I never fail how will I ever _____.'
    a) Complete
    b) Live
    c) Learn
    d) Survive

17. Which Nobel Laureate said: '...let us always meet each other with smile, for the smile is the beginning of love'?
    a) Mother Teresa
    b) Amartya Sen
    c) C.V. Raman
    d) Rabindranath Tagore

18. On being captured and asked by Alexander the Great as to how he should be treated, who said: '...like a king'?
    a) Porus
    b) Ambhi
    c) Ashoka
    d) Chandragupta Maurya

19. Which prime minister said: '...every drop of my blood will invigorate India and strengthen it'?
    a) Indira Gandhi

b) Jawaharlal Nehru
c) Lal Bahadur Shastri
d) Rajiv Gandhi

20. Name the person who said: 'India is the cradle of the human race, the birthplace of human speech, the mother of history, the grandmother of legend, and the great grand mother of tradition.'
    a) Mark Twain
    b) George Orwell
    c) Charles Dickens
    d) Rudyard Kipling

21. 'India has always had a strange way with her conquerors. In defeat, she beckons them in, then slowly seduces, assimilates and transforms them.' Whose words are these?
    a) William Dalrymple
    b) Mark Tully
    c) E.M. Forster
    d) Arthur C. Clarke

22. Who said: 'If Independence is granted to India, power will go to the hands of rascals, rogues, freebooters; all Indian leaders will be of low calibre and men of straw...'?
    a) Winston Churchill
    b) Queen Elizabeth II
    c) Adolf Hitler
    d) Harry S. Truman

23. Who coined the slogan: 'Jai Jawan, Jai Kisan, Jai Vigyan' after the Pokhran tests in 1998?
    a) Atal Bihari Vajpayee
    b) Sonia Gandhi
    c) K.R. Narayanan
    d) L.K. Advani

24. Who said, 'A country's greatness lies in its undying ideals of love and sacrifice that inspire the mothers of the race'?
    a) Sarojini Naidu
    b) Subhas Chandra Bose
    c) Rukmini Devi Arundale
    d) Jawaharlal Nehru

25. 'Time ho gaya hai! Pack Up!' were the last words of which actor?
    a) Raj Kapoor
    b) Dev Anand
    c) Rajesh Khanna
    d) Rajendra Kumar

WILDERNESS

1. In which national park in India was Project Tiger first launched?
   a) Silent Valley
   b) Gir
   c) Kaziranga
   d) Corbett

2. Which of these are the only apes found in India?
   a) Eastern gorillas
   b) Orangutans
   c) Western hoolock gibbons and the eastern hoolock gibbons
   d) Bonobos

3. Which of these is the state animal of Jammu and Kashmir?
   a) Mithun
   b) Hangul
   c) Giant squirrel
   d) One-horned rhinoceros

4. Conservationist Romulus Whitaker established a society in 1978 for the welfare of the Irula community. What is the profession of the community?
   a) Catching snakes
   b) Catching fish
   c) Hunting tigers

d) Collecting medicinal plants

5. Which animal, officially discovered in 1801, is nearly blind and hunts by emitting ultrasonic sounds that bounce off of fishes and other preys?
   a) Stingray
   b) Shark
   c) Gharial
   d) Ganges river dolphin

6. What is the common name of Ailurus fulgens found in Sikkim, West Bengal, Meghalaya and Arunachal Pradesh?
   a) Indian pangolin
   b) Nilgiri thar
   c) Snow leopard
   d) Red panda

7. The Eravikulam National Park has the highest density and largest-surviving population of...
   a) Indian wild ass
   b) Nilgiri thar
   c) Hangul
   d) Red panda

8. Which of these animals lives on the phumdi, the local name for floating marshes on Loktak Lake?
   a) Sangai
   b) Khur
   c) Blackbuck
   d) Indian muntjac

9. Eqquus hemionus khur only occurs in and around...
   a) The Little Rann of Kutch
   b) Dachigam Wildlife Sanctuary
   c) Sunderbans National Park
   d) Kaziranga National Park

10. In India, what is produced from Changthangi and Chegu breeds of goats?
    a) Pashmina
    b) Mohair
    c) Merino wool
    d) Shahtoosh

11. The greater flamingo is the state bird of...
    a) Meghalaya
    b) Tamil Nadu
    c) Gujarat
    d) Goa

12. In 2014, the Kaiser-i-Hind (Teinoplaspus imperialis) was photographed live for the first time in India. What kind of a creature is it?
    a) Spider
    b) Butterfly
    c) Scorpion
    d) Praying mantis

13. What is the National Heritage Animal of India?
    a) Elephant
    b) Hippopotamus
    c) Rhinoceros
    d) Giraffe

14. In Mizoram, the flowering of which plant triggered a boom in the rat population resulting in the 'mautam' famine?
    a) Bamboo
    b) Mango
    c) Coconut
    d) Neem

15. Which animal is referred to as the 'red wolf' and the 'whistling dog'?
    a) Dingo
    b) Dhole
    c) Sangai
    d) Chinkara

16. White teak is the state tree of...
    a) Meghalaya
    b) Jammu and Kashmir
    c) Karnataka
    d) Rajasthan

17. According to a report published by the Botanical Survey of India in 2016, which state has the most species of endemic flowering plants?
    a) Tamil Nadu
    b) Rajasthan
    c) Arunachal Pradesh
    d) Bihar

18. Which conservationist was called the 'Tiger Man of India'?
    a) Salim Ali

b) Fateh Singh Rathore
c) Bibhuti Lahkar
d) Jim Corbett

19. Which animal gets its name from the Indian word for 'pot' because of a bulbous knob at the end of its snout?
    a) Gharial
    b) Mithun
    c) Cheetah
    d) Hangul

20. The Keoladeo National Park, a wintering site of the critically endangered Siberian crane, is located in which state of India?
    a) Karnataka
    b) Rajasthan
    c) Arunachal Pradesh
    d) Tamil Nadu

21. The Chipko Movement was an organized resistance to the destruction of forests in the 1970s. What does the word 'chipko' mean?
    a) Hugging
    b) Felling
    c) Painting
    d) Marrying

22. Apart from Indian cobra, common krait and saw-scaled viper, which of the following is one of the 'Big Four' deadliest snakes of India?
    a) Indian rock python

b) Russell's viper
c) Hump-nosed pit viper
d) Yellow-lipped sea krait

23. Which of these animals is also known as 'Indian Bison'?
    a) Sangai
    b) Gaur
    c) Hangul
    d) Sambar

24. Lakhs of which of these creatures visit the beaches of Odisha for 'arribada' or mass nesting?
    a) Purple crabs
    b) Sea eagles
    c) Olive ridley turtles
    d) Green puddle frogs

25. Which of these does the Muduvar tribe of the Nigiris use to calculate age?
    a) Solar eclipse
    b) The blossoming of the kurinji
    c) Rings on tree trunks of oak trees
    d) Kumbh Mela

X-FACTOR

1. Who was awarded an Honorary Oscar at the 64th Academy Awards?
   a) Bimal Roy
   b) Satyajit Ray
   c) Yash Chopra
   d) Shyam Benegal

2. The United Nations proclaimed which day as the International Day of Yoga?
   a) 1 Feburary
   b) 21 June
   c) 15 August
   d) 22 December

3. In 2014, the World Health Organization (WHO) certified India as free of...
   a) Typhoid
   b) Polio
   c) Cholera
   d) Tuberculosis

4. NAVIC, India's own Global Positioning System (GPS), stands for Navigation with Indian...
   a) Corridor
   b) Communication
   c) Constellation
   d) Channel

5. In which Indian state is the highest cricket ground in the world situated?
   a) Uttar Pradesh
   b) Punjab
   c) Himachal Pradesh
   d) Uttarakhand

6. The national anthem of which country was composed by Rabindranath Tagore's student, Ananda Samarakoon?
   a) Bangladesh
   b) Nepal
   c) Sri Lanka
   d) Pakistan

7. For which book did Kiran Desai win the Man Booker Prize in 2006?
   a) *Hullabaloo in the Guava Orchard*
   b) *The Inheritance of Loss*
   c) *Clear Light of Day*
   d) *Cry, The Peacock*

8. In 2017, India created history by successfully launching 104 satellites on a single mission. From which space centre was it launched?
   a) Balasore
   b) Thiruvananthapuram
   c) Sriharikota
   d) Madurai

9. India won the ICC World Cup in 2011. Who was adjudged Man of the Tournament?

a) Yuvraj Singh
b) M.S. Dhoni
c) Virat Kohli
d) Sachin Tendulkar

10. Which Indian received the Nobel Prize the year Henri La Fontaine won the Nobel Prize for Peace?
    a) Rabindranath Tagore
    b) C.V. Raman
    c) Mother Teresa
    d) Amartya Sen

11. Who was awarded the National Humanities Medal by Barack Obama for her/his 'beautifully wrought narratives of estrangement and belonging'?
    a) Kiran Desai
    b) Jhumpa Lahiri
    c) Anita Desai
    d) Amitav Ghosh

12. Who was the first Indian actor to get a wax statue at Madame Tussaud's in London?
    a) Amitabh Bachchan
    b) Dilip Kumar
    c) Dev Anand
    d) Rajinikanth

13. Which student of IIT Kharagpur went on to become the CEO of Google Inc., 20 years after he graduated from college?
    a) Sundar Pichai
    b) Satya Nadella

c) Sanjay K. Jha
   d) Shantanu Narayen

14. In 2014, India had over 1,54,882...
   a) Universities
   b) Airports
   c) Libraries
   d) Post offices

15. His birth anniversary, 22 December, is celebrated as National Mathematics Day in India. The film *The Man Who Knew Infinity* is based on his life. Who is being talked about here?
   a) Prasanta Chandra Mahalanobis
   b) J.C. Bose
   c) C.V. Raman
   d) Srinivasa Ramanujan

16. According to a report published in 2015, which Indian organization is the eighth biggest employer in the world?
   a) Indian Railways
   b) Indian Air Force
   c) State Bank of India
   d) Indian Oil Corporation

17. Who was the first Indian to win an individual gold medal at the Olympics?
   a) Rajyavardhan Singh Rathore
   b) Mary Kom
   c) Vijender Singh
   d) Abhinav Bindra

18. Who flew on board Soyuz T-11 with 2 cosmonauts Yuri Malyshev and Gennady Strekalov?
    a) Rakesh Sharma
    b) Sunita Williams
    c) Kalpana Chawla
    d) S. Chandrasekhar

19. Who was the first Indian-American astronaut and the first India-born woman in space?
    a) Mohana Singh
    b) Kalpana Chawla
    c) Sunita Williams
    d) Bhawana Kanth

20. Who is the first Asian woman to win the Miss World title?
    a) Reita Faria
    b) Yukta Mookhey
    c) Aishwarya Rai
    d) Celina Jaitly

21. Which national park is the only natural habitat of Asiatic Lions?
    a) Ranthambore National Park
    b) Kaziranga National Park
    c) Gir National Park
    d) Jim Corbett National Park

22. Who won the online reader's poll for TIME Person of the Year in 2016?
    a) Shah Rukh Khan
    b) Priyanka Chopra

c) A.R. Rahman
　　　d) Narendra Modi

23. In 1951, India hosted the first…
    a) Commonwealth Games
    b) Olympics
    c) FIFA World Cup
    d) Asian Games

24. Who became the first woman IPS officer of India in the year 1972?
    a) Bhawana Kanth
    b) Chanda Kochhar
    c) Kiran Bedi
    d) Vimla Mehra

25. Who won a Nobel Prize 'for his work on the scattering of light and for the discovery of the effect named after him'?
    a) Venkatraman Ramakrishnan
    b) C.V. Raman
    c) Har Gobind Khorana
    d) Kailash Satyarthi

YESTERDAY, ONCE MORE

1. In which veda has the Earth been honoured as a Mother: 'Mata Bhumi Putroham Prithivyah'?
   a) Atharva Veda
   b) Rig Veda
   c) Yajur Veda
   d) Sama Veda

2. Nalanda University, which served as a centre of knowledge for more than 800 years, is located in...
   a) Uttar Pradesh
   b) Bihar
   c) Odisha
   d) Rajasthan

3. Which event in the Mahabharata marked the end of the Dwaparayuga and the beginning of the Kaliyuga?
   a) Birth of Bhishma
   b) The game of dice
   c) Life at the court of Virata
   d) War of Kurukshetra

4. Who was the prime minister of United Kingdom when India became independent?
   a) Clement Attlee
   b) Winston Churchill
   c) Harold Macmillan
   d) Neville Chamberlain

5. Which of these is a lyric poem by Kalidasa?
   a) *Ṛtusaṃhāra*
   b) *Malavikagnimitram*
   c) *Vikramōrvaśīyam*
   d) *Abhijñānaśākuntalam*

6. The Mahaparinirvana-sutra describes the last days of...
   a) Gautama Buddha
   b) Mahavira
   c) Guru Nanak
   d) Krishna

7. Who was the first person to sail directly from Europe to India?
   a) John Cabot
   b) Francis Drake
   c) Christopher Columbus
   d) Vasco da Gama

8. Which was the first dynasty of the Delhi Sultanate?
   a) Khilji
   b) Slave
   c) Sayyid
   d) Tughlaq

9. On whose birth anniversary is the National Education Day celebrated in India?
   a) Maulana Abul Kalam Azad
   b) Vallabhbhai Patel
   c) S. Radhakrishnan
   d) Lala Lajpat Rai

10. Which of these cities was given to King Charles II of England as part of his huge dowry when he married Catherine of Braganza in 1661?
    a) Calcutta
    b) Bombay
    c) Madras
    d) Hyderabad

11. Where would you be if you were visiting a village lying east of the Bhagirathi River, about 130 kilometres north of Kolkata?
    a) Buxar
    b) Plassey
    c) Haldighati
    d) Jhansi

12. Who was invited by Daulat Khan Lodi to invade North India in 1524?
    a) Babur
    b) Nadir Shah
    c) Mahmud of Ghazni
    d) Tamerlane

13. In which present-day country was Buddha born?
    a) India
    b) Nepal
    c) Bhutan
    d) Bangladesh

14. According to the Latin historian Justin, a boy (who later became a great king) offended Alexander and was ordered to be put to death. Name the boy?

a) Chandragupta Maurya
   b) Rana Pratap
   c) Shashanka
   d) Prithviraj Chauhan

15. In 1883, who defended Surendranath Bannerjee in the famous contempt of court case against him in the Calcutta High Court?
   a) Womesh Chandra Bonnerjee
   b) Sri Aurobindo
   c) Romesh Chunder Dutt
   d) Rash Behari Ghosh

16. In 1336, which independent kingdom was founded by Harihar and Bukka between the Krishna and Tungabhadra?
   a) Bahmani Kingdom
   b) Vijayanagar Empire
   c) Pratihara Kingdom
   d) Chalukya Empire

17. Who conceived the idea of creating a central place of worship for the Sikhs?
   a) Guru Tegh Bahadur
   b) Guru Ramdas
   c) Guru Arjan Sahib
   d) Guru Amardas

18. His mother, Fakhr-un-nisa, had visited a Muslim saint's tomb in Arcot and prayed for a son. When he was born in 1750, she named him after the saint. Who among the following is being talked about?

a) Jahangir
b) Tipu Sultan
c) Ibrahim Lodi
d) Sher Shah Suri

19. Who was raised under the guardianship of an able Brahmin named Dadaji Khonddev?
a) Krishnadev Raya
b) Shivaji
c) Mihir Bhoja
d) Prithviraj Chauhan

20. Who was defeated by the brave Rajput chiefs of northern India headed by Prithvi Raj Chauhan in the First Battle of Tarain in AD 1191?
a) Qutb ud-Din Aibak
b) Muhammad Ghori
c) Ghyasuddin Tughlaq
d) Khizar Khan

21. Who erected 12 towering altars on the Hyphasis to mark the limit of his march in India?
a) Nadir Shah
b) Mahmud of Ghazni
c) Lord Clive
d) Alexander the Great

22. In his autobiography, about whom did Mahatma Gandhi write: '…was as the Ganges. One could have a refreshing bath in the holy river.'?
a) Gopal Krishna Gokhale
b) Bal Gangadhar Tilak

c) Lala Lajpat Rai
   d) Dadabhai Naoroji

23. Who or what did the Afghan ruler Shah Shuja give Ranjit Singh in return for his help?
    a) River Kabul
    b) Qutb ud-Din Aibak
    c) Peacock Throne
    d) Kohinoor Diamond

24. Which former prime minister wrote *Glimpses of World History*?
    a) Indira Gandhi
    b) Jawaharlal Nehru
    c) Manmohan Singh
    d) Atal Bihari Vajpayee

25. Who was the first vice president of independent India?
    a) S. Radhakrishnan
    b) Vallabhbhai Patel
    c) Maulana Abul Kalam Azad
    d) Bhimrao Ramji Ambedkar

ZERO HOUR

1. In 2009, who became the first woman speaker of the Lok Sabha?
   a) Sumitra Mahajan
   b) Meira Kumar
   c) Najma Heptullah
   d) Mamata Banerjee

2. The 2017 Union Budget was, for the first time, presented...
   a) On 1 February
   b) By the prime minister of India
   c) At midnight
   d) In the Supreme Court of India

3. In the state emblem of India, which of these words would you find below the abacus?
   a) Vande Mataram
   b) Satyameva Jayate
   c) Sare Jahan Se Achcha
   d) Jai Hind

4. Which former president of India was the project director of India's first indigenous Satellite Launch Vehicle (SLV-III)?
   a) Atal Bihari Vajpayee
   b) A.P.J. Abdul Kalam
   c) Pratibha Patil
   d) V.V. Giri

5. What is the maximum strength of the Rajya Sabha is according to Article 80 of the Constitution of India?
   a) 200
   b) 250
   c) 312
   d) 350

6. Who was the first woman-nominated member of the Rajya Sabha?
   a) Rukmini Devi Arundale
   b) Fathema Ismail
   c) Ela Bhatt
   d) Shakuntala Paranjpye

7. Who is the author of *The Hindu View of Life and Indian Philosophy*?
   a) A.P.J. Abdul Kalam
   b) Neelam Sanjiva Reddy
   c) Rajendra Prasad
   d) S. Radhakrishnan

8. Which is the only Union Territory to have a High Court of its own?
   a) Puducherry
   b) Chandigarh
   c) New Delhi
   d) Lakshadweep

9. Who was the first minister of Law and Justice in Independent India?
   a) Mahatma Gandhi
   b) Vallabhbhai Patel

c) Maulana Abul Kalam Azad
d) B.R. Ambedkar

10. The concept of Directive Principles of State Policy was borrowed from the Constitution of which country?
    a) USA
    b) France
    c) Ireland
    d) Germany

11. What is the minimum age for a person to be chosen as a member of the Lok Sabha?
    a) 18 years
    b) 25 years
    c) 30 years
    d) 40 years

12. In which year was the Constitution of India adopted?
    a) 1946
    b) 1947
    c) 1949
    d) 1950

13. Who was the first non-congress prime minister since Independence?
    a) Morarji Desai
    b) Charan Singh
    c) Chandra Shekhar
    d) Atal Bihari Vajpayee

14. Which state sends the most number of members to

the Rajya Sabha?
a) West Bengal
b) Bihar
c) Karnataka
d) Uttar Pradesh

15. During whose term as prime minister was president's rule imposed the most number of times?
a) Indira Gandhi
b) P.V. Narasimha Rao
c) Rajiv Gandhi
d) V.P. Singh

16. Which state does Article 370 deal with?
a) Jammu and Kashmir
b) Arunachal Pradesh
c) Rajasthan
d) Tripura

17. The first woman to serve as the governor of a state in India was the governor of...
a) Bihar
b) Uttar Pradesh
c) Tamil Nadu
d) West Bengal

18. Who was the minister of Finance from 2009 to 2012?
a) Pranab Mukherjee
b) A.P.J. Abdul Kalam
c) K.R. Narayanan
d) Pratibha Patil

19. Until 1958, which of these functioned from the Parliament House till it moved to its present location?
    a) Reserve Bank of India
    b) The Supreme Court of India
    c) Indian Space Research Organization
    d) Union Public Service Commission

20. Who is also the minister-in-charge of the Department of Atomic Energy in India?
    a) President of India
    b) Prime minister of India
    c) Chief Justice of Supreme Court
    d) Vice president of India

21. Who, apart from Edwin Lutyens, designed the Parliament House?
    a) Sir Herbert Baker
    b) Le Corbusier
    c) Charles Correa
    d) Fariborz Sahba

22. Who is the ex-officio chairman of the Rajya Sabha?
    a) Prime minister of India
    b) President of India
    c) Vice president of India
    d) Chief Justice of Supreme Court

23. Who presented the first budget for the Republic of India?
    a) R.K. Shanmukham Chetty
    b) K.C. Neogy

c) John Mathai
d) T.T. Krishnamachari

24. Who among these was the interim prime minister on 2 occasions?
    a) Charan Singh
    b) Chandra Shekhar
    c) V.P. Singh
    d) Gulzarilal Nanda

25. What does Part III of the Constitution of India deal with?
    a) Fundamental Rights
    b) The Union and Its Territory
    c) Citizenship
    d) The States

ANSWERS

AMAZING INDIA

1. Taj Mahal
2. Mamluk
3. Golden Temple
4. Charminar
5. Sun Temple, Konark
6. Victoria Memorial
7. Hyderabad
8. Ghoom Railway Station
9. Sanchi
10. Gateway of India
11. Golconda Fort
12. Konark
13. Mehrangarh Fort
14. Jainism
15. Rashtrapati Bhavan
16. Dilwara Temples
17. Gwalior Fort
18. Karnataka
19. Nalanda
20. Akbar
21. Bara Imambara
22. Jaisalmer Fort
23. Kamakhya Temple
24. Hawa Mahal
25. India Gate

BLUE CHIP

1. Harishchandra
2. USA
3. Konark Chakra
4. C.K. Prahalad
5. BHIM
6. *Stay Hungry, Stay Foolish*
7. West Bengal
8. Sita
9. Kohinoor Diamond
10. Amul Girl
11. Lion
12. Shivaji
13. Palanquin bearers
14. Mahatma Gandhi
15. Ballot boxes
16. Vistara
17. Amartya Sen
18. Shah Rukh Khan
19. Mangalyaan
20. *Raghuvaṃśa*
21. Sensex
22. Tiger
23. *Chanakya*
24. Mumbai Dabbawala
25. SpiceJet planes

CONNECTING INDIA

1. P.V. Sindhu
2. Indian Army

3. Kerala
4. Jyoti Basu
5. *Dainik Jagran*
6. Rahul Gandhi
7. 11
8. Rajiv Gandhi
9. Hike
10. *Meghdoot*
11. Twinkle Khanna
12. Project Arrow
13. UNESCO
14. Himachal Pradesh
15. Pratima Puri
16. Chennai
17. Che Guevara
18. Satyam Shivam Sundaram
19. Zee TV
20. *Indian Opinion*
21. Orbit
22. Dal Lake
23. *Hello*
24. Desh Ka Apna Channel
25. VSNL

DRESSING UP

1. Footwear
2. Kashmir
3. Bhanu Athaiya
4. Paithani
5. Nose

6. Maharashtra
7. Manish Malhotra
8. Tangaliya
9. Japi
10. Mekhela Chador
11. Hand
12. Jodhpur
13. Kanjeevaram
14. Mizoram
15. Jawaharlal Nehru
16. Panetar
17. Mehndi
18. Lepcha
19. Kohl
20. Chandèri
21. Wooden bobbins
22. Anarkali
23. Roosi
24. Muga
25. A knee-length coat

ENABLING INDIA

1. ISRO
2. IIT Kharagpur
3. Tembhli
4. Burma
5. National Cadet Corps
6. All India Institute of Medical Sciences
7. Indian Army
8. Blue

9. Andaman and Nicobar
10. Duty unto Death
11. Vikram Sarabhai
12. Rapid
13. Central Reserve Police Force
14. National Institute of Design
15. Surat
16. Eagle
17. Homi Jehangir Bhabha
18. Netaji Subhas National Institute of Sports
19. C.V. Raman
20. Indo-Tibetan Border Police Force
21. Satyendranath Tagore
22. Chennai
23. Vinod Khanna
24. New Delhi
25. CBI

FULL TOSS

1. Lala Amarnath
2. Sachin Tendulkar
3. Ravi Shastri and M.L. Jaisimha
4. Harbhajan Singh
5. Brazil
6. Suresh Raina
7. Pravin Tambe
8. Navjot Singh Sidhu
9. Rahul Dravid
10. Yuvraj Singh
11. Mohammad Azharuddin

12. K.L. Rahul
13. Ravichandran Ashwin
14. Virender Sehwag
15. Ajinkya Rahane
16. New Delhi
17. Sunil Gavaskar
18. Mohinder Amarnath
19. Virat Kohli
20. M.S. Dhoni
21. Irfan Pathan
22. Bapu Nadkarni
23. Gundappa Viswanath
24. Nayan Mongia
25. Karun Nair

GOURMET

1. Kulfi
2. Hot chillies
3. Kakori
4. Fish
5. Vindaloo
6. Hing
7. Khandvi
8. Guava
9. Modak
10. Khichdi
11. Dum Pukht
12. Rasgulla
13. Maharashtra
14. Dhansak

15. Roti
16. Hyderabadi Haleem
17. Saffron
18. Apple
19. Tamarind
20. Pav
21. Nanfus
22. A slice of bread
23. Undhiyu
24. Coffee
25. Dal Makhani

HOUSEFULL

1. *Dilwale Dulhania Le Jayenge*
2. Priyanka Chopra
3. Raj Kapoor and Nargis
4. *Bhaag Milkha Bhaag*
5. Dev Anand
6. Amitabh Bachchan
7. Rahul
8. *Pather Panchali*
9. Rajesh Khanna
10. Rajinikanth
11. *Saawariya*
12. *Lage Raho Munna Bhai*
13. *Jab Tak Hai Jaan*
14. *Mother India*
15. Karan Johar
16. Dilip Kumar
17. Raja Harishchandra

18. *Sholay*
19. *Alam Ara*
20. *Manthan*
21. Kundan Shah
22. Bhupen Hazarika
23. 3D film
24. Aamir Khan
25. Madhubala

INCREDIBLE INDIA

1. S. Radhakrishnan
2. Kolkata
3. Hsūan Tsang
4. Gujarat
5. Dussala
6. Ravi Shankar
7. Jean Renoir
8. Ronald Ross
9. Gandhinagar
10. R.K. Laxman
11. Tamil
12. Crude oil
13. Horse
14. Dadra and Nagar Haveli
15. All India Radio
16. Maroon
17. Godavari
18. Unani
19. Taj Mahal
20. Qutb ud-Din Aibak

21. Rudyard Kipling
22. New Delhi
23. Bhima
24. Red Fort
25. Lal Bahadur Shastri

JUKEBOX

1. A.R. Rahman
2. M.S. Subbulakshmi
3. Lata Mangeshkar
4. Arijit Singh
5. 'Suno Suno Aye Duniya Walon Bapu Ki Ye Amar Kahani'
6. *Devdas*
7. Ilayaraja
8. Mohit Chauhan
9. Jagjit Singh
10. Pele
11. Shankar Mahadevan
12. Asha Bhosle
13. Sitar
14. Shiv Kumar Sharma
15. Tappa
16. Zakir Hussain
17. Amjad Ali Khan
18. Tabla
19. R.D. Burman
20. Mahatma Gandhi
21. George Harrison
22. Bismillah Khan

23. Tansen
24. Uttar Pradesh
25. Kishore Kumar

KNOW ALL

1. Pune
2. Mughal School
3. Sister Nivedita
4. Bharatendu Harishchandra
5. King George V
6. Palm
7. Jaya
8. Madhya Pradesh
9. Satyajit Ray
10. Shanti Swarup Bhatnagar
11. Uttar Pradesh
12. Narendra Modi
13. The rupee symbol
14. Tripura
15. Lal Bahadur Shastri
16. Meghnad Saha
17. Madan Mohan Malaviya
18. Tamil
19. V. Kurien
20. Chandigarh
21. Gujarat
22. George Orwell
23. Vikram Sarabhai
24. Gandhari
25. Bharatanatyam

LANDSCAPE

1. Gujarat
2. Chhota Nagpur
3. Pakistan
4. Ganga
5. Ten Degree Channel
6. Coromandel Coast
7. Nagpur
8. Regur
9. Barren Island
10. Chicken's Neck
11. Lakshadweep
12. Karakoram
13. Jonha
14. Dal Lake
15. Manipur
16. Rajasthan
17. Kangchenjunga
18. Meghalaya
19. Lonar Lake
20. West Bengal
21. Majuli
22. Drass
23. Jammu and Kashmir
24. Dodabetta
25. Beas

MIXED BAG

1. Graham Greene
2. William Jones

3. Kites
4. Qutub ud-Din Aibak
5. Rajasthan
6. Banyan
7. Saffron
8. U.N. Brahmachari
9. Gandhiji's visit to AIR
10. Pran
11. Coal
12. Kathakali
13. 24
14. Smile
15. Parashurama
16. Amir Khusrau
17. Mango
18. Sanskrit
19. Reserve Bank of India
20. Bara Imambara
21. West Bengal
22. Radha and Krishna
23. Chaitra
24. Mahasweta Devi
25. Agra

NEXT-DOOR NEIGHBOURS
1. Afghanistan
2. Sri Lanka
3. Brahmaputra
4. Buddha
5. Bangladesh

6. Afghan
7. Lal Bahadur Shastri
8. Rabindranath Tagore
9. Tenzing Norgay
10. Bangladesh
11. Aung San Suu Kyi
12. *Raees*
13. Jacqueline Fernandez
14. M.S. Dhoni
15. Abdul Hafeez Kardar
16. Bal Gangadhar Tilak
17. *Train to Pakistan*
18. Fa Hien
19. Bangladesh
20. Sania Mirza
21. Mauritius
22. Khan Abdul Ghaffar Khan
23. Bhutan
24. Jigme Khesar Namgyel Wangchuck
25. Burmese

OUTSTANDING PERFORMANCES

1. Designing the Param Vir Chakra medal
2. 14 November
3. Padma Bhushan
4. Pullela Gopichand
5. ISRO
6. Dronacharya Award
7. Jeevan Raksha Padak Awards
8. Clare Awards

9. Hindi
10. 15 August
11. Ashapurna Devi
12. Shanti Swarup Bhatnagar Prize
13. Music
14. Boxing
15. *The Guide*
16. Shaurya Chakra
17. Eklavya Awards
18. *Do Bigha Zamin*
19. Indian cinema
20. Sachin Tendulkar
21. Gujarat
22. Rajat Kamal
23. Peepal
24. Hindi poetry
25. Ashok Chakra

PLAY OFF

1. Leander Paes
2. Calcutta
3. Ranchi Rays
4. Indian Railways
5. Kabaddi
6. Manjeet Chillar
7. Yogeshwar Dutt
8. Poona
9. Indian Hockey Team
10. Mary Kom
11. P.T. Usha

12. Shot Put
13. Mohammed Ali Qamar
14. Sunil Chhetri
15. Deepika Kumari
16. Rugby
17. Sania Mirza
18. Kabaddi
19. Jwala Gutta
20. Saina Nehwal
21. Viswanathan Anand
22. Prakash Padukone
23. Mohammedan Sporting
24. Dhyan Chand
25. Mallakhamb

QUILL PEN

1. Krishnadevaraya
2. *Flood of Fire*
3. *Bharat Vidhata*
4. *Gitanjali*
5. *Panchatantra*
6. Tamil
7. Rajendra Prasad
8. Sarojini Naidu
9. Firaq Gorakhpuri
10. *Jugnu*
11. Khushwant Singh
12. Munshi Premchand
13. Amrita Pritam
14. Rabindranath Tagore

15. Rama
16. Vikram Seth
17. *Bhagavad Gita*
18. Mahadevi Varma
19. *Silappatikaram*
20. Vijay Tendulkar
21. *Meghdoot*
22. *Kick*
23. E.M. Forster
24. *Mahatma*
25. *Anandamath*

REMARKABLE WOMEN

1. Rajasthan
2. Sunita Williams
3. Dipika Pallikal
4. Lata Mangeshkar
5. Be crowned Miss World
6. Sarojini Naidu
7. Lahore
8. Devika Rani
9. Razia Sultan
10. Anjum Chopra
11. The Mother
12. Sushmita Sen
13. Chennai
14. Manikarnika
15. Vijaya Lakshmi Pandit
16. *Interpreter of Maladies*
17. 'Brimful of Asha'

18. Kiran Bedi
19. Chanda Kochhar
20. Saina Nehwal
21. Priyanka Chopra
22. Mother Teresa
23. Indira Gandhi
24. Maharani Gayatri Devi of Jaipur
25. Bachendri Pal

STATE OF THE ART

1. Chikankari
2. Buddha
3. Thewa artwork
4. Toys
5. Tanjore
6. Akbar
7. Embroidery
8. Karnataka
9. Textile printing
10. Jamini Roy
11. Ajanta caves
12. Khatamband
13. M.F. Husain
14. Ikat
15. Thanjavur Veena
16. Pipli
17. Nek Chand
18. Raja Sawant Singh and Bani Thani
19. Common Man
20. Tying and dyeing

21. Raja Ravi Varma
22. Maharashtra
23. Minakari
24. Phad painting
25. Assamese

TAKE OFF

1. Mumbai
2. White
3. Deccan Odyssey
4. Subhas Chandra Bose
5. Catamaran
6. 10
7. Houseboats
8. *Trains*
9. Bengaluru
10. Ashoka
11. Elephant
12. *Mr and Mrs Iyer*
13. *A Passage to India*
14. Air India
15. Major District Road
16. *Caravan*
17. Swami Vivekananda
18. Fairy Queen
19. Sarojini Naidu
20. Veer Savarkar
21. Horse carriage
22. Munshi Premchand
23. Kolkata

24. Chhatrapati Shivaji Maharaj Terminus
25. Bengaluru

UNITY IN DIVERSITY

1. Phool Waalon Ki Sair
2. Gudi Padwa
3. Nagaland
4. Dashami
5. Cattle fair
6. Breaking the fast
7. Rajasthan
8. Guru Gobind Singh
9. Good Friday
10. Lohri
12. To boil
13. January
14. Gujarat
15. Ladakh
16. Jagannath Temple
17. *Hymn for the Weekend*
18. Kala Ghoda Arts Festival
19. Bikaner
20. Bohag
21. Surajkund International Crafts Mela
22. Karnataka
23. Nashik
24. Shawwal
25. Buddha

VOICES

1. Count
2. Bhagat Singh
3. Max Mueller
4. Spinning wheel
5. J.R.D. Tata
6. Jawaharlal Nehru
7. Charles Dickens
8. Success, failure
9. Lala Lajpat Rai
10. Romain Rolland
11. Chicago
12. Satyajit Ray
13. Subhas Chandra Bose
14. Excellence
15. Mahatma Gandhi
16. Learn
17. Mother Teresa
18. Porus
19. Indira Gandhi
20. Mark Twain
21. William Dalrymple
22. Winston Churchill
23. Atal Bihari Vajpayee
24. Sarojini Naidu
25. Rajesh Khanna

WILDERNESS

1. Corbett
2. Western hoolock gibbons and the eastern hoolock gibbons

3. Hangul
4. Catching snakes
5. Ganges river dolphin
6. Red Panda
7. Nilgiri thar
8. Sangai
9. The Little Rann of Kutch
10. Pashmina
11. Gujarat
12. Butterfly
13. Elephant
14. Bamboo
15. Dhole
16. Meghalaya
17. Tamil Nadu
18. Fateh Singh Rathore
19. Gharial
20. Rajasthan
21. Hugging
22. Russell's viper
23. Gaur
24. Olive ridley turtles
25. The blossoming of the kurinji

X-FACTOR

1. Satyajit Ray
2. 21 June
3. Polio
4. Constellation
5. Himachal Pradesh

6. Sri Lanka
7. *The Inheritance of Loss*
8. Sriharikota
9. Yuvraj Singh
10. Rabindranath Tagore
11. Jhumpa Lahiri
12. Amitabh Bachchan
13. Sundar Pichai
14. Post offices
15. Srinivasa Ramanujan
16. Indian Railways
17. Abhinav Bindra
18. Rakesh Sharma
19. Kalpana Chawla
20. Reita Faria
21. Gir National Park
22. Narendra Modi
23. Asian Games
24. Kiran Bedi
25. C.V. Raman

YESTERDAY, ONCE MORE

1. Atharva Veda
2. Bihar
3. War of Kurukshetra
4. Clement Attlee
5. *Ṛtusaṃhāra*
6. Gautama Buddha
7. Vasco da Gama
8. Slave

9. Maulana Abul Kalam Azad
10. Bombay
11. Plassey
12. Babur
13. Nepal
14. Chandragupta Maurya
15. Womesh Chandra Bonnerjee
16. Vijayanagar Empire
17. Guru Arjan Sahib
18. Tipu Sultan
19. Shivaji
20. Muhammad Ghori
21. Alexander the Great
22. Gopal Krishna Gokhale
23. Kohinoor Diamond
24. Jawaharlal Nehru
25. S. Radhakrishnan

ZERO HOUR

1. Meira Kumar
2. On 1 February
3. Satyameva Jayate
4. A.P.J. Abdul Kalam
5. 250
6. Rukmini Devi Arundale
7. S. Radhakrishnan
8. New Delhi
9. B.R. Ambedkar
10. Ireland
11. 25 years

12. 1949
13. Morarji Desai
14. Uttar Pradesh
15. Indira Gandhi
16. Jammu and Kashmir
17. Uttar Pradesh
18. Pranab Mukherjee
19. The Supreme Court of India
20. Prime minister of India
21. Sir Herbert Baker
22. Vice president of India
23. John Mathai
24. Gulzarilal Nanda
25. Fundamental Rights

15/4/23